Podcasting

52 brilliantideas

one good idea can change your life...

Podcasting

The ultimate starter kit

Steve Shipside

CAREFUL NOW

Nothing moves faster than a new medium and when that medium is hosted on the World Wide Web there's a whole host of unknowns to play with. Web addresses change so if a link doesn't work then you'll have to look around (try Google). Podcasts that were funny go stale; portals go in and out of fashion; podcasts come and go altogether; and, most of all, with no censorship out there podcasts frequently feature language fit to make a shock jock blush. So, take care. Likewise you should have a virus checker installed if you are going to download anything whatsoever and you should be aware that new applications may squabble and bicker with old ones, causing glitches in your system. We're very sorry about all this and wish it was a better world but it's the only one we have. We believe in taking it on the chin like grown ups and expect you to do the same. We love you dearly but if it all goes kumquat shaped then you're on your own; we take no liability. See it as an adventure.

Copyright © The Infinite Ideas Company Limited, 2005

The right of Steve Shipside to be identified as the author of this book has been asserted in accordance with the Copyright, Designs and Patents Act 1988.

First published in 2005 by
The Infinite Ideas Company Limited
36 St Giles
Oxford
OX1 3LD
United Kingdom
www.infideas.com

A CIP catalogue record for this book is available from the British Library.

ISBN 1-904902-73-1

Designed and typeset by Baseline Arts Ltd, Oxford
Cover designed by Cylinder, Suffolk
Cover image © David Medina Claesson/iStockphoto.com
Printed by TJ International, Cornwall
Podcasting disc created by New Media Army,
www.newmediaarmy.ca

Brilliant ideas

Introduction

Podcasting is all things to all people. To the BBC it is an opportunity to free listeners from the shackles of schedules and, by doing so, reach out to an audience that otherwise misses out on quality radio. To the commercial radio stations it offers a chance to claw back that generation which has largely abandoned the radio in favour of iPods and Playstations. To thousands of people with something to say but no budget for broadcasting it means a chance to get their message across on an equal footing with the big boys. For thousands of others it's a media free-for-all in which any adolescent in Ohio can take to the mike, make his or her own show and have the satisfaction of knowing it is being heard all over the world.

With so many different approaches to the medium it is hardly surprising that the result is a bit of a jungle, but then that's part of the appeal. With podcast portals helping to sift through the explosion of broadcasts by listing popularity charts (www.podcastalley.com) or quality criteria (www.podcastbunker.com), it is becoming easier to filter and select podcasts. You don't have to listen to 'my first cassette recorder' style hooting unless you want to. Big media companies like Virgin, Disney and Bravo are already producing professional podcasts for your pleasure and Apple's inclusion of podcasting within the latest version of iTunes sets the seal on its mainstream credentials. So, if it's polished podcasts you're after, take your pick.

At the same time, the fact that it's nearly free to roll your own means that there is plenty of room for the experiments, the fringe, the minorities, the esoteric, indeed the weird and wonderful of every kind, so it's unlikely that podcasting is going to become dull anytime soon. The idea of this book is to give you a taster of what's out there and, in the process, introduce you to some of the best sites to get hold of what you like. There are some tips for playing back your podcasts on a wide variety of podcast-friendly devices, and some pointers for that day when you start to think 'Why not me? Why don't I record a podcast?' Hopefully there's something for everyone. Enjoy.

Note about URLs
The easiest way to find podcasts is to go to a podcast portal (see Idea 2, *Take me to your podcast*). Many podcasts have their own website separate from their 'feed' (where you subscribe). Where there is a website with more information about the podcast then that URL is given and the feed can be found on it. Where there doesn't seem to be extra information about the podcast then the feed address may be the only one given.

1

Invasion of the pod people

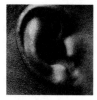

Why the fuss over podcasting?

In October 2004, a Google search would have returned fewer than 6000 results for 'podcasting'. By August 2005 that number had risen to over ten million results – a reflection of the growing interest in the new medium. So what's all the fuss about?

Defining idea

'**Podcast** noun: *a digital recording of a radio broadcast or similar programme made available on the Internet for downloading to a personal audio player.*'
One of the new additions to the *Oxford English Dictionary*, 2005 edition.

According to research company TheDiffusion Group, the 840,000 Americans who listened to podcasts in 2004 will grow to 56 million by 2010, and by then three quarters of those who own digital music players will be listening to podcasts. Steve Jobs, founder of Apple Computer, describes podcasting as 'the hottest thing going in radio'.

The fuss is two-fold. Firstly, in terms of existing radio broadcasts, it makes the break away from a fixed time schedule. Instead you download your favourite show to your computer or mp3 player and listen to it at your leisure – on the way home, in the subway, or the next day.

The other part of the promise is that, unlike most radio, a basic podcast can be put together and made public with nothing more than a computer, an Internet account and a cheap microphone. Anyone with something to say (and more than a few without even that) can now become a broadcaster and say what they like, regardless of commercial restraints, government censorship or funding (or talent, as the more critical will note).

That has seen a transition whereby blogging – essentially diaries written on the web – has gone audio and become podcasting (the name comes from Apple's iPod mp3 player). Podcasting is currently a largely amateur occupation giving voice to those who would otherwise be neglected by mainstream media. If you have a hobby, an obsession, or just a bit of time on your hands you could join them. 'It's about real people saying real things and communicating,' according to Adam Curry, the former MTV VJ and chief cheerleader of podcasting – the podfather himself.

According to Curry the advertising and corporate radio companies are deeply threatened by this groundswell of do-it-yourself digital media but it is the destiny of digital media to start off on the fringe and move steadily into the mainstream. Already the likes of Disney,

Virgin and Bravo are experimenting with podcasting and some of the best quality material is from old stalwarts like the BBC. Podcasting in one shape or another is coming to a device near you and the list of podcast-friendly devices already includes mp3 players, mobile phones, computers and even a pair of sunglasses. Whether as a consumer or a creator, it's time to get with the podcast people.

Here's an idea for you

For an idea of just how much podcasting is out there and how fast it is growing, point your browser to Podcast Alley (www.podcastalley.com) and look for the Site Statistics box on the home page. Podcast Alley doesn't claim to be an exhaustive list, and there are many podcasts that it doesn't know of, but as of summer 2005, at the point Apple's iTunes version 4.9 was released, this site alone listed 5,731 podcasts featuring over 96,000 episodes.

2

Take me to your podcast

Where to find them

Type 'podcasting' into Google and you get about ten million responses. Given that (at time of writing) there are reckoned to be about ten thousand actual podcasts, that makes for a lot of junk to sift through before you even find a podcast, let alone one worth listening to. So try these ideas instead.

Defining idea

'Broadcasting is really too important to be left to the broadcasters.'
TONY BENN, British politician

For a start try getting your podcast software to do the donkey-work for you. Not all pod software works the same way but many of the more popular ones, such as iPodder, come up with a tab you can click on marked 'Podcast directory'. Click on that and as long as you are online it will scan for collections of podcasts grouped together under categories. Signing up from here on is as simple as clicking on the one you want and following the instructions.

If your podcast software doesn't oblige with a directory listing, or if you want to take the time to browse around the available podcasts, then by far the best approach is to tootle off to the podcast portals (websites that consist of links to available podcasts). Here are some examples.

iPodder

iPodder is best known as an 'aggregator' (the bit of software that goes and subscribes to podcasts for you) but also exists as a portal you can visit on the web. Categories tend to be a bit catch-all and there are no notes to guide your choice but there is a decent range at:

www.ipodder.org

Podcast Alley

This one's worth knowing about because it is effectively a hit parade of podcasts. It not only lists by the usual categories but also features a listener voting system so you can see at a glance what's hot and what's not. Now and again you might suspect that listing success owes more to a podcaster's friends and family than any critical judgement but at least you get a general idea of what the world is listening to.

www.podcastalley.com

Podcast Pickle

Stupid name, good site. Podcast Pickle not only has a more helpful directory than most (it's not rocket science, just better use of subcategories) but also includes links out to websites as well as feeds so you can get an impression of a podcast before you sign up to download the thing.

www.podcastpickle.com

Podcasting News

As the name suggests, this is more a site for news about podcasting than a directory of podcasts themselves (though it does that too). However, it does throw up a fair selection of new and interesting sites.

www.podcastingnews.com

Podscope

The idea of search engines dedicated to podcasts is a great one but Podscope is in its infancy and it's a little early to say whether it will fulfil its promise of delving through web-wide audio files to find what you want.

www.podscope.com

Here's an idea for you

Why not really enter into the spirit of things and try a podcast that rates other podcasts? The Podcast Directory is itself a fine portal (www.podcastdirectory.com) but the Podcast Directory podcast is even better because the folks from the directory rate and review their way through the plethora of podcasts on offer.

www.wolfdatasystems.com/podcast.xml

3

Podcasting to your PC

You don't need an iPod, Apples are not the only fruit, and, no, you don't even need an mp3 player. Podcasting and PCs go together perfectly, thank you.

Defining idea

'A computer once beat me at chess, but it was no match for me at kick boxing.'
EMO PHILIPS, US comic

Got a PC? Got an Internet connection? Then unless you bought your computer as army surplus from the Napoleonic wars, it's ready to download and listen to podcasts.

All you need to be able to do is get yourself online and grab podcasts using a piece of software that goes out, signs up for the podcasts you want, and downloads them to your PC. It's much like downloading music except that instead of clicking a button and getting one song, podcasting is about subscribing to a series of broadcasts so the software that does that needs to know and do a little more. The essential thing is to find your podcast (see IDEA 2, *Take me to your podcast*), tell your podcatcher software where to go to look for more, and schedule it so it knows how often it should take a peek to see if the next episode is ready. It then downloads the file to your computer (just where exactly depends on which folder you opt to have the software download to) where it's ready for you to play by clicking on it. To play basic podcasts you need nothing more complex than Windows Media Player, which came included in your copy of Windows.

There are dozens of different podcatchers available for the PC, including:

iPodder (*www.ipodder.org*)
Doppler (*www.dopplerradio.net*)
RSS Radio (*www.dorada.co.uk*)
iTunes (*www.apple.com*) and
Nimiq (*www.nimiq.nl*)

to name but a few. They all do essentially the same thing, which is to allow you to subscribe to a podcast that they then check for updates and download new episodes from as appropriate. To be honest, a lot of the difference is simply taste. Apple's iTunes is getting all the attention right now, although its directory listings are not as extensive as some of the more established podcasters. It's also a tad on the bulky side compared to more stripped-down applications like RSS Radio, which is easy to use but doesn't direct you straight into listings and so involves more cutting and pasting of web addresses.

Some, such as Doppler, are dependent on other software components, notably Microsoft's .NET. Downloading the one may entail downloading and updating the other, which can be a pain. Probably the best approach is to download a couple and see which you like the best.

Here's an idea for you

While Apple's iTunes is generally raved about, not least because it links directly into the online music store, it may not be the best for you if podcasting is first and foremost what you do online, and downloading music is an afterthought. iPodder, on the other hand, was created by podfather Adam Curry and opens up with expandable menus of podcasts on offer, sorted by genre, which it updates whenever you fire it up. Currently at least it features many more podcasts than iTunes and if something catches your eye you just click on it.

www.ipodder.org

4

Podcast that Mac

With the fuss over iTunes you might be forgiven for thinking there is only one podcasting application for the Mac, and the trio of iTunes, iPod and Mac is a hard one to beat. It's not, however, the only game in town.

There's no doubting the importance of iTunes 4.9 to the development of podcasting, and while a Windows Media Podcast Player and a RealMedia Podcaster are set to follow as sure as night follows day, it's our fruity friends at Apple who have stolen a march with the new medium.

iTunes Podcast Library is a perfect place to find new podcasts and the simplicity of clicking on the Get button is the easiest way yet of subscribing to them. Other podcatchers were there first, however, and some are prepared to put up a fight for their turf, notably iPodderX.

The kind of things that iPodderX offers include the ability to keep an eye on those fast-breeding podcasts in the form of SmartSpace – a utility that lets you specify just how much of your precious hard drive space you'd like to have populated by old podcasts. iPodderX can automatically delete the old files. That's more useful than you'd think because one of the problems with podcatchers (including iTunes) is that they tend to show only new files – which is great except that it means that old ones are sometimes left lying around ignored, making the place untidy.

iPodderX goes beyond the capabilities of iTunes in the amount of different data types it can handle, including photos (it integrates with iPhoto), but best of all is the way it handles text. Text streams were where RSS (Really Simple Syndication) started out as users subscribed to news feeds to have headlines or articles automatically downloaded to their desktops. iPodderX can do that but better yet a utility called NewsCaster takes that text news and converts it to speech so it reads the news back to you. This means that it can take a stream of text – say financial results, for example – and turn it into an audio file for you to listen to on your way to work. That alone makes it worth a look.

Here's an idea for you

Podcatchers are free, easy to download and don't (usually) conflict with each other so you can have your cake and eat it by downloading several and trying them all to find your own favourite. Aside from iTunes, the ones you should check out include:

iPodderX (http://ipodderx.com/) – see above,

iPodder (http://ipodder.sourceforge.net/index.php) – The Podfather's own and truly multi-platform,

NewsMacPro (www.thinkmac.co.uk/newsmacpro/) – supports podcasting with Palm and iPod sync,

Playpod (www.iggsoftware.com/playpod/) – designed for Mac OS X.

5

Podcasting on the hoof

Podcasts to your mp3 player

Just about everything seems to be an mp3 player these days – keyrings, watches, jewellery and sunglasses have all been equipped with just enough memory to serve up songs. Good news for podcasters.

The mp3 format is ten years old. It has ushered in music downloading, transformed music players and is the driving force behind digital audio today. The curious thing is that it's taken ten years to find out that what it's really best at is podcasting.

MP3 is a success because it makes music manageable; so manageable that it can be played on must-have shiny tiny players. It does that by compression – basically squeezing those lardy music tracks into svelte, lithe, easy-to-handle files.

The amount it squeezes those files is variable and is known as the bit rate. A higher bit rate means better quality but fatter files and vice versa for a lower rate. The bit rate required for near-CD audio (called 128 KB) will only squeeze an hour of music into 64 MB of memory; lower quality can fit much more in. Enter the podcast.

If you've always got the latest and greatest of everything then your mp3 player probably boasts more MB of storage than NASA. If you've got an old one collecting dust somewhere it may only have 64 MB of memory. That's an hour, tops, of music. But it's a whole load more podcasting pleasure. FM quality audio (half the bit rate of CD audio) will fit two full hours of listening into that same amount of memory. AM quality takes that up to a glorious four hours. Typically, podcasts such as the popular Dawn and Drew show aim for a bit rate equivalent to FM radio. Speech alone can be done with less, though, and so the BBC, for example, opts for somewhere in between AM and FM quality, giving you about three and a quarter hours of beautifully enunciated podcasting from the cheapest, oldest mp3 player you can find.

While mp3 players usually lack the sophisticated autofill and syncing features of, say, an iPod hooked up to iTunes, they are still perfect for podcast playing. It is less elegant to plug the mp3 into a computer and manually drag and drop your chosen podcasts over to it, but a couple of minutes will set you up with hours of listening, even from your old steam-powered mp3 player.

Here's an idea for you

Not only do you not need an iPod to enjoy podcasting, but you can enjoy podcasting on the hoof for less than the cost of a pair of iPod headphones. Presuming you already have access to a computer to download your podcasts, all you need is the cheapest, simplest mp3 player to play them back. Go to eBay and you'll find new mp3 players on sale for less than ten pounds (fifteen euros or dollars), and sometimes half that. Since podcasts themselves are free, that means hours of listening pleasure while you jog or journey for less than the cost of lunch.

www.ebay.com

6

It's for you-hoo

Podcasts to your phone

Forget the Crazy Frog – you can download more to a phone than novelty ring tones and now that phones are emerging with more memory and the ability to play mp3 files they are starting to be used as podcast players.

Defining idea

'That's an amazing invention, but who would ever want to use one of them?'
RUTHERFORD B. HAYES, nineteenth US president on having just witnessed a test of the telephone in 1876.

The idea of just having one device that fulfils the functions of phone, music player and radio is appealing, not least to the handset manufacturers who seem hell bent on beefing up your handset until it becomes a full-on multimedia machine. Along with built-in cameras and light sabres, modern phones are fast acquiring large amounts of memory that can be used for mp3 files, and that in turn makes them podcast capable.

The amount of memory available tends to be the sticking point at the moment because phones aren't usually blessed with gigabytes of the stuff. Then again, the lower data demands of podcasts mean that a small amount of memory goes much further when filled with podcasting rather than with music. The cheap headphones that tend to come with mp3 phones are also much better suited to talk radio podcasts than they are to quality music.

One tip for you is that while smaller amounts of memory mean you may be happy to transfer podcasts across to the phone one at a time, once you get into the habit of regular podcast listening it's time to learn about smart playlists. iTunes and other podcatchers such as iPodderX can create playlists of music for you to upload all in one go. One better is the Smart Playlist that can be configured to swap new podcasts for old every day but there is a slight catch. Out of the box (as it were) iTunes 4.9 doesn't allow you to set up Smart Playlist for podcasts. Instead you'll have to move the folder containing your podcasts into the general library if you want to be able to sort them as you would your music.

Where it really starts to get interesting is with the new generation of phones, such as the Sony Ericsson W600. They are rewriting all the rules, with stereo speakers and the ability to store up to ten full-length CDs and access the Internet. At that point even the mighty iPod starts to find itself with competition.

Here's an idea for you

Alan Joyce at Everythingdigital.org has created an application, PodcastToPhone, which looks for your phone playlist on the Mac and then automatically sends it to your mobile phone via Bluetooth File Exchange. It's a free application, downloadable from his site and while currently only available as a Mac version he is continuing to work on new versions of the application so it's worth a look at his site, and a listen to his blog, to see how he's getting along with it.

www.everythingdigital.org/

7

Podcasting and iTunes

Defining idea

'Really easy to find these podcasts, really easy to listen to them.'
STEVE JOBS, Apple CEO, on the launch of iTunes 4.9

Having decided that podcasting is the 'hottest thing going in radio', Apple Computer set out to make it even easier to get hold of and listen to podcasts. How? By building it right into iTunes.

What Apple has done with the latest version of iTunes (v4.9) is to take the various different elements of finding, retrieving and listening to podcasts, and put them all together into one piece of software. Devastatingly simple, but someone had to think of it.

Where podcasting normally requires users to install 'podcatcher' software, which goes out and subscribes to podcasts, iTunes has rolled the podcatcher into its music download software, making signing up as easy as clicking a button. The results were immediate, with listeners signing up for more than a million podcasts in just the first two days of iTunes featuring them.

With iTunes installed you need only go to Podcast (it's listed at the top of the Source window on the left-hand side) and the podcast interface pops up. From there you will find the podcast directory with thousands of podcasts ready to go. To subscribe to a podcast feed you need only look under the Advanced menu options of the main iTunes menu and there you will find 'Subscribe to Podcast', which calls up a URL box to type or paste your chosen podcast RSS entry into.

Enfolding podcasting into iTunes has undoubtedly made it easier to find and listen to podcasts, so much so that, as Steve Jobs comments, 'we think it's going to basically take the podcasting mainstream'. Not all of the pioneers of podcasting are too happy about that – the news that the likes of Disney and Bravo are appearing in the podcast directories has sparked a fear that the mainstream will muscle in. It's a big web out there, though, and as long as there's server space the chances are that every kind of taste will be catered for – however weird, wonderful or wacko.

iTunes, in case you're not familiar with it, exists mainly to promote the iTunes Store, through which you can pay for individual tracks or albums that you download. This caused some worry amongst podcasters that Apple would start to charge for something which has to date been downloadable gratis. Jobs insists that this is not the case and that podcasts accessed through iTunes will continually be free – after all, it all drives demand through the iTunes network and helps fill up those iPods.

Here's an idea for you

Do you think you need a Mac to set up iTunes? Well, you don't – there's a Windows version available for download from the same site. At 21 Mbytes, it's a hefty download, but worth it to benefit from the user-friendly Apple interface and the all-in-one management and subscription tools. Oh, alright then, truth is it's worth it just to be able to display its stainless-steel chic on your desktop – in design terms alone it makes most of the home-grown PC applications look like old word processors. iTunes for Mac and Windows ('Radio Reborn') is at:

www.apple.com/itunes/download/

8

Rip, mix, burn, podcast

The iPod in all this

The iPod is to digital audio what the Walkman was to the cassette player and, while you don't have to have one for podcasting, there are millions of us out there sporting those little white earplugs.

Defining idea

'You've got to deal with the devil. Let's have a look. The devil here is a bunch of creative minds, more creative than a lot of people in rock bands. The lead singer is Steve Jobs. These men have helped design the most beautiful object art in music culture since the electric guitar. That's the iPod.'
BONO, lead singer with U2, on associating the band with a product.

Podcasting owes its name to the iPod, and with iTunes 4.9 bringing so much to the podcast party there's more reason than ever for that.

For a start you can sync directly to the iPod and do so with a series of preferences so that you choose which podcast episodes you want to update – all of them, selected ones, recent ones, or unplayed ones. That works well when your subscription lists start to build up and you need to manage a large number of different programme episodes.

If you listen to part of a podcast, then play music, then go back to the podcast it will pick up where you left off. Sync to your iPod and the same is true even if you start listening on your computer, then sync, then carry on listening on the iPod. One word of warning, though: if you want this to work then don't set the 'Podcast Preference' in iTunes to only keep the unplayed episodes. Do that and any partly listened-to podcasts will be treated as unwanted leftovers and binned rather than saved to nibble on later.

You may have to update your iPod's software to benefit from these features. Download an iPod updater from www.apple.com and it will decide for you if it needs to update.

Notice that the Autofill function of iTunes won't work if you want to fill up your iPod with podcasts; nor can you create a 'Smart Playlist' of podcasts and if you select 'Shuffle Songs' you won't see podcasts appearing in the mix. That's because podcasts live in the 'Podcasts' folder, a different iTunes playlist from the main Library. If you want to create smart playlists of podcasts, or generally have your iPod treat them the way it does music, then you'll need to move the Podcasts folder into your Library by dragging it over from Finder (Mac) or Windows Explorer (PC). If you do this, then you can still see your podcasts separately with the purple podcasts master playlist icon on the right, but iTunes will otherwise treat podcasts the way it always managed your music.

Here's an idea for you

Play your iPod podcasts through your car stereo. There are three ways to hook the two systems up:

- A cassette adapter that looks like an old-fashioned cassette but has a jack your iPod plugs into (needs a cassette deck in the car to work).

- An FM transmitter, which turns your iPod into a (very) local radio station that you listen to on your radio (cheap but variable quality due to interference).

- A dedicated connection kit (specific to a certain car stereo and may have to be installed by the maker but guaranteed quality).

9

Enhanced podcasts

Chapter, verse and photos

Podcasting is already evolving into enhanced podcasts, which allow you to include pictures, chapter information and even slide shows to accompany the audio.

Enhanced podcasts are encoded audio files with the inclusion of other data (images, text, etc.) at certain points along their timeline. That means that as the audio plays you can have appropriate pictures appear, or have subtitles, or a web address that complements what's being said or sung. They also include chapters, which means that you can break a podcast down and skip from one chapter to another without having to play the whole podcast. Put together, that turns each individual podcast into a multimedia presentation and potentially a great tool for teaching or entertainment.

When you play an enhanced podcast in iTunes, a little icon of a book pops up at the top of the window in between the rewind/play/forward buttons and the running time display. Click on that and a menu pops up, displaying the chapters, images and other information of the podcast. There may also be artwork in the podcast, which you won't see if you don't have the artwork window open. To find the artwork window take a look at the bottom left-hand corner of iTunes, where there are the 'Playlist', 'Shuffle' and 'Repeat' buttons. The next one along is a pop-up menu box with a standard menu icon but click on it and the artwork display window opens up underneath your playlists. (Note: Mac OS X 10.2.x users won't see artwork in the pop-up menu, but everything else works the same.)

If you play enhanced podcasts on an iPod it will show the title of the chapter you're listening to but if you load up enhanced podcasts onto any mp3 player with just the standard display you won't get to see the artworks, pictures, slideshows etc. Just like video podcasts, it can't turn a dedicated audio device into a video one. That's worth bearing in mind if you're thinking of making enhanced podcasts because while more fully functioned players like Macs and PCs will benefit, it only adds another layer of complexity for simpler devices to stumble on.

If you're curious about what an enhanced podcast looks like, Apple invites you to go to the iTunes Music Store and subscribe to the iTunes *New Music Weekly* podcast.

Here's an idea for you

If you fancy making your own enhanced podcasts, or if you're the sort of person who likes to pull things apart in order to understand them better, then take a look at *Make Magazine*, which features Phillip Torrone's definitive tutorial on making your own. It's clear, it's step-by-step and it's gloriously geeky, right down to the pictures of wire strippers and electrical tape (not themselves required for making podcasts).

www.makezine.com/blog/archive/2005/07/how_to_make_enh.html

10

You ain't seen nothing yet

Video podcasts

Radio is only the beginning for
podcasting because the blogs
(online diaries) that paved the way
for podcasts have themselves
already started to evolve into vlogs (video logs). Magazine-
style programming is already sprouting video.

Defining idea

*'A film is just like a muffin. You make
it. You put it on the table.'*
DENZEL WASHINGTON

The principle of vidcasting or video logging, or vlogging, as it is
variously known is not technically any different from normal
podcasting. The shows are made and posted with the RSS link,
which means you can subscribe and download new episodes as they
appear. The difference is just that these files contain video and
because that makes them bigger downloads each episode is
normally much smaller. Where typical podcasts are half an hour or
more long, the typical video podcast will usually be only a few
minutes and that affects the kinds of subject matter they treat.

While some of the video is predictably amateur, the time constraints mean that a lot more thought goes into content and presentation with the result that certain of the video podcasts out there are textbook examples of minimal visual storytelling. Tune into some nuggets.

Tiki Bar TV

It's got exotic drinks, occasional yodelling, gloriously kitsch backgrounds, rubber faced gurning and bizarre characters striding in and talking darkly of offending the Tiki gods. Glorious. Tiki Bar TV consists of short episodes of cocktail mixing in a swank bachelor pad but that's where the logic runs out. A videocast to watch while wearing a smoking jacket and a fez and sipping something with an olive in it.

http://feeds.feedburner.com/TikiBarTV

DIVB-TV

The Dumbass Idiots Video Blog is a vlog of people doing or saying mind-blowingly stupid things in a kind of sub-*Jackass* format. Some funny, some just Dumbass Idiotic.

feed: http://feeds.feedburner.com/DumbassVideos

Rocketboom

Three-minute daily video blog from the Big Apple covering quirky to mainstream news and based around anchorwoman Amanda Congdon. The result is funny, well done, and has caused a lot of fuss amongst more traditional big-budget news organisations looking to learn from the quality/cost ratio of Rocketboom's production.

feed:
www.rocketboom.com/vlog/quicktime_daily_enclosures.xml

Vlog of a Faux Journalist

'Multimedia as Literature' is the subtitle of this site and with a mix of media including short poetry films about cinematography this is one from the arty end of the vlogging spectrum.

http://feeds.feedburner.com/diaryofafauxjournalist

Xolo TV

Filtering out the ab fab from the fabulously awful is going to be a big job with vlogging so why not let someone else do the dirty work? Xolo TV is a weekly review of the good, the bad and the ugly from the world of video blogging.

www.xolo.tv

Here's an idea for you

Got an old iPod (first or second generation) gathering dust somewhere? Want to turn it into a video player? Well you can, although it involves updating the device in a way that will void the warranty so it's absolutely not recommended for a new device or one where the warranty is still valid. The trick is to install a Linux operating system in the form of iPodLinux. All the software and tools you need to teach your old pod new tricks can be found at

www.ipodlinux.org/Main_Page.

It's not too techy, it doesn't stop you listening to your old music, and it will bring a new lease of life to the small screen of an old iPod.

11

When podcasts go bad

Common problems

Podcasts are simplicity themselves, right up until they aren't and your computer refuses to play ball. Here are some of the problems you may find.

Defining idea

'All progress is precarious, and the solution of one problem brings us face to face with another problem.'
MARTIN LUTHER KING, Jr.

Q: I downloaded some podcatcher software but, when I try to install it, all I get is an error message about missing components.

A: You could spend hours trying to update little snippets of software with incomprehensible names like Active-X and .NET but realistically the easiest thing is probably to download a different podcatcher and try again. Try the tried and trusted big names like iTunes, or iPodder.

Q: Where'd they go?

A: Your podcast software has spent all day downloading but you can't find anything to show for it? You need to find out where you have set the software to download to. If you're using iPodder or similar then look for the 'Preferences' menu (usually part of the 'File' menu) which will tell you where any downloaded podcasts are going. If all else fails try using the 'Search' function and searching for *.mp3 files. That will usually ferret them out.

Q: Where did all my old podcasts go?
A: If you're using iTunes then it will ask to import all your existing music into iTunes to manage it more easily. This is great but remember that any applications you used before iTunes may not be able to find them again after the move.

Q: And my new iTunes podcasts?
A: Similarly, if you're using iTunes and moving your podcasts to an iPod, then one of the options you can choose is 'Delete original after moving'. If you choose that then the podcast only exists on your iPod and iTunes or iPodderX won't be able to find them to play them.

Q: You said there are hundreds of podcasts at this site but iTunes only shows one.
A: The podcast feed (that confusing line of text that ends in '.rss') only points to the latest podcast – which is how podcasters know if there's a new one. iTunes doesn't display any of the previous ones, just the latest. Have a rootle around the podcast site to find older ones which may have been stored separately under the heading of 'archive'.

Q: Why is my podcast not working for others?

A: If your mp3 file plays just fine for you, but doesn't work when you upload it as a podcast, you might want to use an automatic feed validator to ensure that the URL and the RSS files all point to the right place and read the way that other computers expect them to. Try http://feedvalidator.org/ or http://audio.weblogs.com/feedDebug.html – just type in the URL for your podcast and hit the 'verify' button.

Here's an idea for you

With Apple now rolling podcasting into iTunes, it is likely to take over the mainstream of podcasting on both Macs and PCs. While the Apple troubleshooting guide for podcasting is still limited compared with its iPod and iPod Shuffle brethren, it is growing and at least provides the answer to why there is a blue dot or an exclamation mark appearing in iTunes next to your podcasts. Check it out:

http:/docs.info.apple.com/article.html?artnum=301880

12

I want my MTV

What you won't hear and why

Right now, podcasting is largely amateur with the mainstream media companies dipping their nervous toes in the water – an attitude that has little to do with corporate conservatism, and a lot to do with legal wranglings. Here's what you won't be hearing for a while.

Podcasting has the potential to give radio a huge shot in the arm and open up an entirely new audience. However, before the traditional world of wireless and the 'wired' generation can truly get it together, a lot of things still need to be settled (not least of which are the lawyers' bills).

Radio stations are coming to podcasting, with examples such as the Pete and Geoff breakfast show in the UK. At the moment, these are podcast without the news, the weather or the music, which might be perfect for Geoff's mum, but for the average listener it seems a bit bare bones. The sticking points are the copyright and serialisation rights of issues like news and weather, and the obvious risk of illegal downloads of music. After all, if you download a podcast of a top-twenty radio show you also have copies of all the music. Even Rush Limbaugh, the self-styled 'industry leader in podcasting' (i.e. he charges for his shows) doesn't deliver the entire show for those who have paid to hear it because he doesn't have permission to play the 'bumpers' (snippets of music). Limbaugh has told his listeners that while he strives to get permission he is 'running up against a brick wall because so much piracy is going on out there'.

All this means it'll be a cold day in hell before you can listen to the top twenty as part of a podcast. In the meantime, most music broadcast in podcasts is what's called 'podsafe' – meaning that it is royalty free or offered up with the permission of the bands concerned. For many podcasters, that's part of the beauty of podding since it gives an experimental, indie feel to the scene that they fear will be lost if podcasts were to go mainstream.

Where the licensing regulations really cause trouble, however, is not just music but the law on sound recordings. The licences for playing recordings were usually agreed directly with the performers while, traditionally, over-the-air (radio) broadcasters haven't had to have a licence to play a recording. The problem is that podcasting, unlike broadcasting, leaves the listener with a copy of the performance, which means it falls under distributing rules rather than broadcasting. This is why you won't get radio soap operas being podcast unless an agreement can be struck with every cast member, or the licensing laws are changed to allow for podcasts (don't hold your breath).

Here's an idea for you

Instead of holding your breath and waiting for MTV to come to podcasting, why not revel in the fringe benefits and look at pod-friendly groups that demand no royalties and deliberately aim to be distributed by podcasting? For a taster of off-the-beaten-track beats you should try the Podsafe Music Network, which has featured artists, sample tracks galore and a host of suggestions of other sites that specialise in music the record labels haven't gotten their grubby paws on yet.

http:/music.podshow.com/

13

Rock my pod!

Mainstream music podcasts

Rock and roll will never die. It will, however, metamorphose into mutually hostile tribes and end up being argued over by fans with all the fervour of inquisitionists. We're not here to take sides, just to suggest a few.

Ben's HardRockCast

You'd have thought that being responsible for the Scorpions would have killed off the German hard rock scene, but no, it looks set to live as long as there is someone to hold a lighter aloft. Weekly reviews of hard rock – and heavy metal – albums and concerts . . . in German.

www.attrax-online.de/podblog/rss.php?kategorie=Metal

Hungbunny

'Words, music, and no f*****g banter' is how the podcast presents itself. It's a showcase of the likes of Primal Scream, Jello Biafra and the Dead Kennedys – not what you'd choose to lull children to sleep by.

http://hungbunny.libsyn.com/rss

KSSX Metal Showcase with Niki

Niki is the American Ben (see above) except that even Ben doesn't seem to have heard of the joys of Alabama Thunderpussy or Cassie Eats Cockroaches.

http://feeds.feedburner.com/kssx

Not Your Usual Bollocks

Why NYUB? 'It's not your usual bollocks . . . because mainstream radio is s**t,' explain the producers. Offbeat and unpredictable, with not a commercial endorsement to be heard.

http://notyourusualbollocks.squarespace.com/

PODMEGO Rock Music

One for the weird box, this, as Podmego specialises in the less well-travelled roads of rock, including a show on Panama's premier rock band, Bajo Zero, and their latest releases. Podmego really gets into its stride, however, when on the trail of such international superstars as 'Monkeypox'. Judging by Monkeypox's debut, 'Hey! That's My Wife!

Get Your Own!', these guys could go far so remember you heard them first on Podmego. Of course it's just as likely that you'll be hearing them last here but that's the risk you take out there on the cutting edge of rock.

http://podmegorock.libsyn.com/rss

The Best of Mikey and Jimmy

Pretty much the opposite of NYUB (above), since Mikey and Jimmy's show is a top-rated music/talk show from Long Island's 1240 WGBB. Only the highlights are podcast but perhaps that should be rebranded as the lowlights since these mainly seem to consist of Mikey and Jimmy getting hog-whimperingly drunk with guest bands in the studio. Funny, if totally unstructured. And drunk.

http://mikeyiztha1.users.blogmatrix.com/podcasts/index.xml

Here's an idea for you

Ever dreamt about being on the road with the band? Well, here's your chance, only without the hangovers and unfortunate rash. Sunspot Road Mania is a front seat in the van as the rock band Sunspot travels around the Midwest in their POS Ford van, bringing you stories from the road and what currently passes for their lives. It's heavy on the music (by Sunspot and others they meet) and whining, not least as the beloved van turns into a sweatbox by midday and the usual bitching between superstars kicks off. But, hey, that's the rock and roll lifestyle for you.

http://feeds.feedburner.com/Sunspot

14

Indie podcasting

Because independent music and podcasting are like peas in a ... erm

Podcasting is one of the cheapest possible ways of distributing new music. For all those indie bands out there, unencumbered by record label contracts and vast amounts of money, podcasting has proved a natural way of getting themselves heard. Here are just a handful of the indie music podcasts waiting to demo themselves to you.

My Virtual Band

It doesn't get much more indie than this. The site myvirtualband.com is a place where online collaboration is encouraged so that musicians and digital music fans anywhere on the web can contribute to the creation of songs. These are then collected together and played on the MVB Radio podcast every couple of weeks. It's unusual, unpredictable and definitely unsigned music from next door and the other side of the planet all at once.

www.myvirtualband.com/

IndiePodcasting.com

IndiePodcasting.com serves up new indie music from the great unsigned. The music is surprisingly high quality and it's a good place to hang out for the 'I was into them before they were famous' brigade.

www.indiepodcasting.com

Insomnia radio

Looking for pop-punk from Portugal? Garage rock from Canada? The freshest of the UK music scene? Insomnia Radio showcases independent music and unsigned acts of all types and tastes. The result is one of the best indie shows available and it's continually experimenting with the format, launching, for example, a short podcast with several diverse tracks in it called Short Attention Span.

www.insomniaradio.net/

iROCK Radio

iROCK is a weekly music podcast featuring 'the best independent music artists from Oklahoma.' Just in case you're worried that this translates to rednecks singing about cattle and divorce, iROCK is quick to point out that the Oklahoman independent music scene does take in rock, hip hop, and more.

http://irokradio.com/

The Sounds in My Head

'A weekly music show featuring songs and bands you might have missed', as it says on the box. I'd go a step further and say that you would definitely have missed the songs in question because even though some have been signed and produced discs they are all from way out in left field. Expect a bizarre and wonderful mix of styles and musical genres of all types. If Rob, the record shop owner from *High Fidelity*, were to do a podcast (and he would), then this is the sort of thing you'd expect him to produce.

http://www.thesoundsinmyhead.com/

Here's an idea for you

Looking for something a bit different in music? Well there are more ways to find the fringe of the mainstream than by sampling the unsigned. Vinyl Podcast is a site by podfather Adam Curry in which he podcasts music from old LPs that have gone past their sell-by date and are no longer published. 'Fair use of forgotten music' is how he describes it and the result is an oddly eclectic selection from the fringe of the music world.

www.vinylpodcast.com/

15

The podcast concertos

Podcasts for classical lovers

The Queen has an iPod, you know, and much as I would like to think that she's spending her time listening to the Sex Pistols I suspect that her tastes may be a little more conservative. That's just fine, because there's room in podcastland for everyone. Here's something for the classical fans.

Music Perspectives

This is the classical music magazine podcast. Very much about the history of classical music, with a blend of sound clips and talks with experts and musicians about the importance and development of, for example, Purcell or Rossini.

http://feeds.feedburner.com/musicperspectives

Naxos

Naxos, long established as *the* name in cheap classical CDs, has launched into the Internet with a vengeance. It has a podcast about new releases, performers and composers, as well as audio samples and information on the Naxos catalogue. The site is www.naxos.com and the podcasts are at:

www.naxos.com/podcasts/naxospodcasts.xml

BBC Specials

While the schedule isn't fixed in stone, the BBC is committed to experimenting with digital audio and as part of that is making downloads available of its major classical music projects. 'The Beethoven experience' features the complete works of the composer with the symphonies performed by the BBC Philharmonic in Manchester and conducted by Gianandrea Noseda. It's available as mp3 files at:

www.bbc.co.uk/radio3

This Is Your Music Classical

While the show claims to be about all great composers, it is clear that the real passion of the hosts is opera and the kind of material to be found includes melodies and discussion about Puccini, Bizet, Mozart and Strauss.

www.multicast-1.com/Radio Central/TIYM/Classical.xml

Podopera

Some believe opera isn't actually all about overpriced boxes, fiddly little binoculars and fancy evening wear. The Hatstand Opera is on a mission to make opera fun and accessible to people of all ages and its director and mezzo-soprano Kirsty Young hosts this collection of interview, previews and chat.

http://podopera.podblaze.com/

Bowed Radio

Here's a one-hour show gorging on the talent and techniques of strings players the world over. It's more of a classical-fest than anything else, but there's still enough variety to keep the resin-wielding fiddling fraternity happy.

http://www2.bowed.org/

Here's an idea for you

For every classical music buff there is also a wannabe podcaster for whom the appeal of classical music is that it is royalty free and thus safe for distribution. Music for Podcasters is a site about other podsafe music available for podcasts at SASmusic.com. It covers classical, jazz, new age, aerobic, cheerleading music and more. The show highlights a special album of 30-second and 60-second intros/outros called 'Podcast Music'. Go listen before podcast music takes over from ringtones as the new top twenty.

www.sasmusic.com/Podcast-01-SASMusic.rss

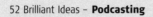

16

ROFL

Podcast comedy

Funny ha ha, funny peculiar – planet podcast has both in bucketfuls, though not everyone agrees which particular casts fall into which category. Here are a few to help you make up your own mind, and remember that if you think you know something funnier then you should let everyone else know about it by voting for that podcast at Podcast Alley (www.podcastalley.com).

Defining idea

'Human life is basically a comedy. Even its tragedies often seem comic to the spectator, and not infrequently they actually have comic touches to the victim. Happiness probably consists largely in the capacity to detect and relish them.'
H. L. MENCKEN, iconic newspaperman

Teknikal Diffikulties

For all I know that's the correct spelling in the 'wilds of Minneapolis', which is where your host, Cayenne Chris Conroy, comes from. Billed as 'fun for the whole family … if the family is a bit on the dodgy side', this is a fairly offbeat collection of grumbles and insights into, well, anything really.

http:/cayenne.libsyn.com/rss/

Keith and the Girl

The dual-presenter format is everywhere in podcasting, and Keith Malley and his girlfriend Chemda are no exception. One of the most listened-to podcasts on the web, they make fun and talk sh** about daily life in the office, in the kitchen, wherever. Keith's home site, by the way, is www.shite.com, which may give you an indication of what you're in for.

http:/keithandthegirl.com/

Nobody Likes Onions

Patrick (the obnoxious one) and Adam (the non-obnoxious one)'s comedy show has been a regular feature in Podcast Alley's top twenty for nearly as long as it has been going. Caustic, straying well into politically incorrect territory, and generous in its sarcasm regarding anything from toothpaste to technology, the show has drawn a lot of criticism, not least from the hard-core faction of onion loving fundamentalists. 'A lot of bad things have been said about our podcast,' muse the boys; 'we've heard that we like to eat babies, we employ Moroccan slave labour, we give out poison apples on Hallowe'en, we killed the last dinosaur in 1996, we mailed the anthrax letters to Congress, etc. The fact is, a couple of those things are just rumours.'

http:/feeds.feedburner.com/nlo

Yeast Radio

Adam Curry, the Grand Old Man of podcasting, once described Yeast Radio by saying, 'It's as if Rush Limbaugh, Joan Rivers and Howard Stern had a mutant lovechild.' To others it has the name because it's a nasty little infection that just won't go away. To find out which side of the fence you fall on, try the feed at:

http://feeds.feedburner.com/yeastradio.xml

Here's an idea for you

The fact that there are no real time restraints means many podcasts overrun or keep going until they dry up. Sometimes, however, short is sweet, particularly when it comes to comedy. If you don't happen to be blessed with abundant bandwidth and just want a quick chuckle then point your browser to Comedy4cast, which crams skits, spoofs and shaggy dog stories into a bijou four-minute format for quick relief.

www.comedy4cast.com/

17

GSOH

Sex, dating and pod porn

As long as there are people to talk, there will be talk about sex. It's not surprising, then, that a number of podcasts have sprung up to cope with the eternal human fascination with making more humans.

Defining idea

'What's nice about my dating life is that I don't have to leave my house. All I have to do is read the paper: I'm marrying Richard Gere, dating Daniel Day-Lewis, parading around with John F. Kennedy, Jr., and even Robert De Niro was in there for a day.'
JULIA ROBERTS

Dating Dynamics – dating advice for men

The Dating Dynamics podcast covers dating advice for men on 'how to get women, and keep them!' This is a series of regular shows, which if the hosts have any decency will be continued until every last bloke is satisfactorily hitched. In the meantime, however, the DD show looks at tips about body language, small talk, confidence-building and the eternal poser of 'why nice guys finish last'.

www.capo2001.podlot.net/

Pod-Porn

Aural sex. Fortunately Pod-Porn spares us the sound effects part of making the beast with two backs and instead focuses on tales of 'debauchery, fidelity, infidelity, fun, and fantasy'. There are no pictures, thank heavens, and those nice people down at Pod-Porn like to think they are producing for 'mature minds' so best quest elsewhere for teenage kicks and cheap thrills.

www.pod-porn.com/

The Sexologist Show

Brigitte, the show explains rather breathlessly, is 'a real sexologist!' (as opposed to the blow-up ones?) who talks about issues of intimacy and sexuality as well as holding 'bed-ins' with guests to talk about their sex lives.

www.thesexologist.com/thesexologist.xml

The Bert and Nena Sex Show

A podcast on sex, dating and gender politics tragically not hosted by Burt Reynolds, as the graphics suggest, but instead by Bert Hughes and Nena Tempelton. Despite this, it's a great discussion forum for things like TV and sexual mores and how to get chicks/birds (this is a bilingual American/British site). Occasionally Bert and Nena interview people in dire need of help with their dating, which has that kind of rubbernecking fascination normally reserved for road accidents.

www.deepsignalstudios.com/podcasts/bnss/

Here's an idea for you

While the site is currently as sparsely populated as a peat bog, PodDate is a fascinating idea that could just take off. Have a listen: it's an Irish dating site that delivers personal singles' ads as audio recorded from their phones and then distributed as podcasts. Singles record a sound message on a computer or any phone equipped with a 'memo recorder' feature then email the clip to PodDate, which screens it for content and publishes it so people can hear what you sound like before deciding to try to get it on. Or you can just get your weirdo kicks from listening to eighteen-year-old Emma ('quite pretty') from Clonmel.

http://poddate.blogsome.com/

18

The big screen in your pocket

Film reviews

Because podcasting is bite-sized entertainment you take around with you, it has quickly been adopted by those looking for information about films and DVDs. Or as the podfather Adam Curry once said (about the Cinecast Show): 'Perfect for the Friday commute to help you decide what you're going to watch over the weekend.'

Reel Reviews

Reel Reviews was one of the earliest review sites and the original format remains constant with a ten-minute episode looking at films to see either on the big screen or to hunt out down at the DVD shop. Encouraged by the response to Reel Reviews, the creator, Michael Geoghegan, has gone on to produce a sibling cast about the silver screen called the Cinephile Series, which consist of half-hour analyses of films past and present. Geoghegan's success in getting himself established is a tribute to the dedicated amateur (he owns an insurance marketing company) and Reel Reviews is more like sitting down with a hard-core film buff for a coffee than tuning in to a professional review show. For many people, this is the entire point of podcasting.

http://reelreviewsradio.com/

(Cool) Shite

This is a downbeat, down under, knockabout podcast about films, films on TV and sometimes just TV. Sometimes cool, sometimes shite.

www.coolshite.net

DVD Weekly Podcast

Home cinema means precisely that for a lot of people: the big screen is in the corner of the room and the DVD release schedule is a lot more relevant than the blockbuster opening days. If that sounds like you then try the weekly DVD podcast that is, erm, DVD Weekly.

www.dvdweeklypodcast.com/

Cinecast

Any site that gets the vote of podfather Adam Curry has to be worth a listen and Cinecast turns out to be a well-informed conversation about films. Rating films is a secondary goal but the podcasters do use a five-star grading system (pinched from Netflix) to help you decide in a hurry whether a film is likely to be a hit or miss. Cinecast features a number of reviewers with varying tastes but between them they cover a wide variety, including a lot more art house and foreign (i.e. non-Hollywood) films than most of the other podcasts.

www.cinecastshow.com/

Here's an idea for you

Mark Kermode of the BBC's Five Live radio show does a series of film reviews that are put out as a podcast. Kermode doesn't attempt to dazzle with his in-depth knowledge of film history and he's seldom prone to gushing, but as a down-to-earth tipster on good films to catch he is easy to listen to and a decent judge of whether a release merits an outing down the movies or is one to mentally file and wait for the DVD to appear on the rental shelves.

www.bbc.co.uk/fivelive/entertainment/kermode.shtml

19

Buy, sell, podcast

Business information on podcast

Because podcasting is all about not being live, there isn't a lot of business news available. What there is instead is a lot of discussion about entrepreneurship, small business and, above all, marketing and communications. In many cases this ends up as more podcasts about podcasts but there are a few, here and there, that stand out.

Boston Globe Bizcast

One of the few relatively mainstream business commentaries, the *Boston Globe* Bizcast is largely the brainchild of one D. C. Denison, who is the technology editor on the *Boston Globe* business staff. Produced weekly, his business and technology podcasts look at winners and losers in the tech arena, interview business leaders, and make good use of the newspaper's own reporters by hauling them in and picking their brains for comments on events.

www.boston.com/business/podcast/

Business Week

Mainstream media are still testing the waters of podcasting and *Business Week* seems slightly embarrassed about it. Certainly it's done a fair job of hiding its budding poddy section deep in the 'Extras' category of the site. A little rooting around turns up a selection of casts, mainly on technology and podcasting itself but also including investing and small business.

www.businessweek.com/search/podcasting.htm

Webmaster Radio

Technophobes look away now. Webmaster is for those who make their livings from websites, whether that be by churning out code to keep sites up to date, fancy footwork around the search engines to keep those same sites in the public eye, or new marketing techniques to turn an honest penny in the process. It's one for the (would be) online entrepreneur aiming to keep in touch with the tricks of the trade.

www.webmasterradio.fm/episodes/show_podcast.php

BLRN Financial News Talk

That's the Bottom Line with Todd Hickman and Gene Vallorani is a financial news radio show that's been on the air since 2002. Both Hickman and Vallorani are registered financial consultants and their double act largely turns around issues of risk, insurance policies and corporate investors.

http://feeds.feedburner.com/BLRNFinancialNewsTalk

For Immediate Release: The Hobson and Holtz Report

For Immediate Release: The Hobson and Holtz Report is a twice-weekly podcast by a duo of 'communication professionals' (a label that covers a multitude of sins) with opinions on marketing and communications. What makes the show different is that Hobson is based in Amsterdam while Holtz hangs out in Concord, California. It's more concerned with new media and podcasting than anything else but the trans-Atlantic gimmick guarantees it a different slant nonetheless

http://forimmediaterelease.biz/

The Podcast Brothers

Despite sounding more like a stand-up comedy act, the Podcast Brothers host a weekly show on the business side of podcasting and portable media. That translates into more podcasting about podcasting but it has a more businesslike slant than most.

www.portablemediaexpo.com/audio.htm

Here's an idea for you

Most podcasts are effectively shameless self-promotion so it's hard not to be tickled by the one business cast that comes out and nails its colours to the computer. Check out Diary of a Shameless Self-Promoter, a podcast entirely about 'effective self-promotion ideas' and hosted by Heidi Miller, a worldwide speaker, corporate presenter and a shameless ... well you get the idea. For all the brashness of the show's title, it does also give space to techniques for more low-key self-promotion and is arguably one of the most apt uses for podcasting on the planet.

http:/heidimiller.libsyn.com/

20

Faster, higher, stronger

Sports podcasting

If you're a big Pittsburgh Steelers, San
Francisco 49ers or Washington Redskins
fan then sports podcasting is a rich
tapestry of delights. Mainstream US
sports are fairly well catered for but
even the lesser known sports (underwater hockey, soccer, etc.)
are out there if you know just where to look.

Defining idea

'Sport is the only entertainment
where, no matter how many times you
go back, you never know the ending.'
NEIL SIMON

Search engines and most of the pod portals tend to favour a couple
of US podcasters, not least for the media attention they have
received to date. Of these, the following ones are those you are most
likely to come across.

SportPodcasts.com

On a mission to build the world's largest sports podcast directory, SportPodcasts.com is the place to be for everything from 'Arsenal America' to 'Barry Bond's knee problems'.

www.sportpodcasts.com/

The Sportspod

Sam Coutin specialises in NFL podcasts but has around five casts on the go at once, including a variety programme and a sports betting podcast with tips on how to beat the bookies. Oddly, Coutin himself has been quoted as saying that sports podcasts have been slow to take off 'because of the lack of a correlation between sports and geekiness'. Football widows may have a few words to say about that.

www.thesportspod.com/

Sports Pod Net

For NBA, NFL and various other acronyms posing as sport.

www.sportspodnet.com/

The Premiership Podcast

It's soccer to those in the US, footie to those in the know and futbol to those who can actually play the game. The Premiership Podcast is about the English Premiership league and, astonishingly, appears to be the only podcast about 'the beautiful game' at time of writing.

(Still, at least that puts it ahead of cricket, about which there seems to be nothing available at all – buck up chaps, what are you waiting for?) Get stuck in (my son) at:

http:/andesmallwood.libsyn.com/rss

5 Speed Cassette

Pro Cycling, Formula 1 racing, indie music and 'random events' are here. According to the producer, 'titanium components were used to ensure that subject matter will never fail due to shifting social pressure'.

http:/falconportal.com/family/podcast.xml

Bike Talk Radio

It's a weekly show about all aspects of cycling.

www.biketalkradio.com/show/podcast/index.xml

ScubaRadio

This is probably best enjoyed in conjunction with IDEA 22, *Podcasts by (and in) the pool: waterproof podcasting solutions.*

www.scubaradio.com/srpodcast.xml

Here's an idea for you

Up the ante on your sports podcasting entertainment by betting your shirt on the basis of something you picked up from an mp3 file. Beats tips from the beery-breathed bloke down the pub. BetUS has been on the go for over a decade and boasts about 100,000 clients – aka 'sporting gents', 'punters' or 'suckers' depending on where you're coming from. It's now making its BetUS radio show available as a podcast so you can listen to head handicapper-honcho Eddie King offering 'wit, betting advice and a raw look into the world of sports betting'. Don't expect any insights into horse, whippet or cockroach racing, but there are insider tips on the usual American acronym sports plus hockey, golf and boxing.

www.BetUS.com

21

All the news that's fit to podcast

Defining idea

'I do not like to get the news, because there has never been an era when so many things were going so right for so many of the wrong persons.'

OGDEN NASH

Well not exactly all the news because, as you may have gathered by now, the things that make podcasting what it is are that (a) it is not 'live' and (b) it is currently dominated by the amateurs and the outlandish. This means that mainstream news is only really starting to dabble with it. On the other hand planet podcasting is a superb place for some very different takes on what should be in the news.

WTOP news

Some traditional news sources are experimenting with podcasts of their news, as for example WTOP news, Washington's all-news station, which has started to create a 15- to 30-minute daily news update for commuters.

www.wtopnews.com

Distorted View Daily

One of a number of podcasts specialising in news of the worldwide weird. Or as Distorted View prefers to put it, 'Come for the news of the weird, stay for the audio pornography!'

www.distortedview.com/show/

Sky News Podcast

Rupert Murdoch's Sky News is another news specialist testing the waters with podcast versions of bulletins. They don't seem to be shouting about it, though, and the website has barely a mention of it so the only way to find out more seems to be to subscribe directly to the site and hear the news from:

http://podcast.burstinteractive.co.uk/rss.xml

Tim Riley's City Desk

Although it's claimed to be news, current events and pop culture stories ignored by the mainstream media, most of the actual information is pretty straightforward lead news stories with a bit of weird stuff thrown in. Bizarrely, Tim Riley ('Portland's most recognised broadcast journalist') reads all this in the style of a 1950's radio announcer telling the world that little green men have landed in Central Park.

www.timrileymedia.com/

P.I.D. (Peering Into Darkness) Radio

Authors Sharon K. Gilbert and Derek P. Gilbert, creators of *The MythArc* series of supernatural thrillers, look beyond the news to present your weekly conspiracy fix. Oh yes, if you want your latest on the Nephilim, Roswell and the new pope, this is the only place to go.

http:/peeringintodarkness.com/radio/pidradio.xml

Here's an idea for you

If you want up-to-the-minute news then a website or radio station is always going to be better than podcasts so it makes sense that the real value of podcasts is to provide the summaries and analysis – in short, podcasts are to news what news magazines are to newspapers. So why not try subscribing to *Newsweek* and listening to its podcast version? The veteran news magazine produces a concise round up of the latest issues, which can be found at:

www.msnbc.msn.com/id/7078547/site/newsweek/

Podcasts by (and in) the pool

Waterproof podcast solutions

What you want to listen to, when you want it, and where you want it, that's the idea of podcasting. Well some people clearly take that to mean by the pool, in the pool, or even under the shower. Here's how.

Defining idea

'Someday we're all gonna dive …
seven tenths and rising.'
Slogan of Seven Tenths divewear.

Waterproof audio is a great idea – think of catching up on business information or taking in a talking book as you lap up the lengths. Or maybe you just want to lie back and let it all flow over you without worrying about your music player going phut. The good news is, you can. There are essentially two ways of taking your podcasts into the waves (without ruining your mp3 player). The first is to go out and buy an entirely waterproof player, the second is to wrap a waterproof casing around your existing one.

iPod by the pool

Since Apple hasn't seen fit to release a sub-aquatic iPod to date, you'll have to look at getting an iPod case if you want to submerge your pod. There are several manufacturers who let you do just that: Lilipod (www.lilipods.com), Otter (www.otterbox.com) and H2O (www.h2oaudio.com) all make waterproof cases with waterproof headphones for iPods and other mp3 players.

Sub-aqua audio

Cases for kit are relatively cheap but have the downside that you will always wonder if it's going to protect your precious player this time as you clip the thing in the box and prepare to take the plunge. A dedicated waterproof player, on the other hand, comes with no such aquatic anxiety. The Finis SwiMP3 (www.finisinc.com/), for example, is built into the swim goggles and consists of a small player that sits on the back of your head and noise inductors that lie flat against your cheekbones. There are no headphones as such; instead the music is transmitted through the bones of the face to the ear (sound quality is unaffected). It's more expensive than the case solutions, but features no trailing wires, was born for the wet and is probably the solution for the serious swimmer.

Cheaper but usually less rugged is the option of a waterproofed flash mp3 player like the Oregon Scientific MP120 (www.oregonscientific.com/), which is small, neat, cheap and includes an FM radio for when you get carried away on your laps and the podcasts run out. These devices use headphones and the cheaper ones don't feature the nice grippy headphones of the more expensive cases but a simple solution that improves sound and keeps bud earphones in place is to wear a swim cap over the top and voila – tunes as you tumble turn.

Here's an idea for you

You want to take this waterproof mp3 to the next level? You're a keen listener to the Bottom Time Radio podcast (www.bottomtimeradio.com)? Then you'll be delighted to know there is one mp3 casing designed to dive deep into Davy Jones's locker so you can podcast with the fishes. It only works with the iRiver 300 series of mp3 players but it has to be the only audio accessory on the market with a clip to attach to your mask strap and a working depth of 60 m (200 ft). Just think, you could download the Jaws theme to it and swim around to the tune of 'duh-dum, duh-dum ...'

www.H20audio.com

23

Pluckthumping

Learning music by podcast

Of all the educational possibilities of podcasting, music and language stand out as the ones with the most to gain from the medium. There is no limit to what music you could learn from podcasts, no limit at all. So what's with all the banjos?

Frailing Banjo Lessons

Anyone who has ever seen *Deliverance* can tell you that banjos are played only by psychotic in-bred hicks prior to doing disgusting things and killing people. It's a fact, so why would anyone want to play banjo? Well, it seems they do and so Frailing Banjo Lessons or, more understandably, 'pluckthumping' as the project was originally called, has come to be podcast. Originally the podcast started as a banjo workshop with 'homework' (you can find it at http://funkyseagull.com/frail-1.mp3) but enough people completed the homework and so the father and son Costello team went ahead with the lessons. In between squealing like piggies, obviously.

http://funkyseagull.com/lesson.xml

VideoDrumLessons.com

Definitely a podcast to hide away from teenage children. The name is misleading because the podcast is audio only but there are lots of drumming tips and info for the aspiring drummer.

www.VideoDrumLessons.com/news/rss2.xml

Explore your voice

Well, you'll get into a lot less trouble than you would exploring someone else's. Singing, whether in bands or drunken karaoke sessions, is discussed here and aims at anyone taking singing lessons. According to the podcasters, the commonest problem people have is deciding if it's going right when there is no teacher in front of them, so there's a lot of emphasis on learning how to feel when it's right.

www.exploreyourvoice.com

Easy Music Theory

Music theory tips and how-to advice from a course that already exists on CD-ROM and the web but has now been reborn as a podcast.

http://easymusictheory.com

Piano Lesson Podcast

A new boy on the block, and not the most originally named, Piano Lesson Podcast promises 'ongoing, online piano lessons delivered directly to your computer, iPod, or other mp3 player. Topics include chord piano playing, play by ear, blues, country, gospel, piano bar and styles'. The site also promises secrets, strategies, exercises and theory for intermediate instant piano playing.

www.pianofun.com/blog1/podcast.html

Here's an idea for you

Actually here's an idea for my neighbour, who can only play the intro to *Smoke on the Water* (and he's not the only one). *Wayne's World* should have been the final nail in the coffin of guitarists who can only play *Stairway to Heaven*, but they're still out there. So, if that sounds like you then do everyone a favour and tune into Matt's Guitar Lick of the Week, where every week he takes one or two of the best licks out there and breaks them down so guitarists everywhere can be slightly less predictable.

website: www.learntoplayrockguitar.com
feed: www.learntoplayrockguitar.com/mattsguitarlickoftheweek.rss

Parlez vous Pod?

Learning languages by podcast

As well as plenty of opportunity to listen to programmes in your chosen language, the podcast panoply includes a fair amount of language learning from those who have realised that teaching the spoken word can't be done by books alone.

Really Learn Spanish

According to the podcaster this is: 'A series of podcasts aimed at helping you in your efforts to learn Spanish using unconventional techniques.' Not sure about the 'unconventional'; however, you can be very sure that the 'real' part of 'really learn' comes through as our teacher includes samples of Spanish spoken badly (usually with a heavy American accent) and then corrects them in a helpful way.

Aimed at adult students, it features more pronunciation tips than most.

http:/radio.weblogs.com/0142338/2005/03/06.html

Trying to Learn Spanish

Personally I think the title sounds like a podcast for those flailing and failing with the language but then that may also be intentional with this programme focusing on reviews and commentaries on available resources, including books and tapes.

http:/feeds.feedburner.com/Tryingtolearnspanishpodcast

Curso De Portugues No Podcast

And you thought it was hard enough getting your tongue around Spanish. You'll need the Kanji character set loaded on your computer or else your screen is liable to be flooded with question marks. On second thoughts, that seems fairly reasonable for a site in which a mixed Japanese/Brazilian explores the world of the Portuguese language.

www.poino.net/radio/index.xml

The PiEcast

The PiEcast is one of the best out there for the main European languages. PiE (Partners in Excellence) is a really great initiative that regularly uploads language learning podcasts for students of

German, French and Spanish. It's intended to be for schools (though it has plenty to offer anyone learning the languages) so it has an eye on the exam season, with appropriate listening exercises posted in time for the aurals. Best of all it aims to catch the attention of those of us who hated traditional language learning and spent most of our time throwing things at each other in the back of the class. Recommended.

www.pie.org.uk/

Ugly Expat

You can't really resist a title like that and our ugly expat teacher of English as a second language really ups the ante by adding a hint of grumpy to the mix. That's a bit rich seeing as how he would appear to be living and working in Hawaii. Opinions and comment on teaching ESL and global politics.

www.uglyexpat.com/

The French Pod Class

French language and culture lessons with a bit of a sing-song thrown in for good measure.

www.frenchpodclass.com/

Here's an idea for you

Kwe sewakwekon, ohnisonhatie? Of course you do. Say what you like about the poor quality and self-indulgence of many podcasts out there but this is the only media that has brought the wonders of Owennii – The Good Word – to my desktop. It's a podcast that helps people learn Kanien'keha. That's Mohawk to you and me, but you probably already knew that. You've got the hairstyle, now learn the language.

http://feeds.feedburner.com/MohawkLanguage

25

Ich bin ein podcaster

Non-English language poddery

Although English has totally dominated podcasting, German is carving itself a surprisingly strong niche. Look around a bit on the sidelines and you'll see that German is a bit of a dominator here, and it's not the only language making its mark.

Defining idea

'That woman speaks eighteen languages and can't say "No" in any of them.'
DOROTHY PARKER

PodBlaster.net

PodBlaster is the number one French site dedicated to French language podcasting. It aims to help put Gallic geeks in touch with an audience worldwide since, as the site admits, 'French podcasters are not yet very numerous'. That said, the site does feature dozens of podcasts in seventeen categories so if you want to work on your French then this is the place to go.

www.PodBlaster.net

Le Podcasteur

No, I tell a lie – if you want to work on your French then this is the place to go, not least because it is such a great name. It's a magazine format about life and music in France.

http://feeds.feedburner.com/BertrandLenotreMultiPodcasting

Carte postale de . . .

A great travelogue in French, the producers create audio postcards of places for you to dream about as you sit waiting for the bus.

http://cpd.galeota.com/feed.xml

RadioNK Caffenichilismo

The primo podcast Italiano, Radio NK has taken the coffee and chat format of so many podcasts and made it a Vespa-fest of Lavazza espresso and excited hand gestures.

www.radionk.com/rss.xml

De Theepod

A spin-off from Dutch radio station Radio Gamba exploring the making of Internet radio.

http://feeds.feedburner.com/theepod

Fluox Speelt Fluox

Fluox is a Dutch chat show talking about pretty much anything but with a particular nod towards 'kinky gezever'. I'm told that 'gezever' is Dutch for going on and on about something but I stand to be corrected if any nerds from the Netherlands say otherwise.

www.fluox.nl/podcast.php

El Bloguipodio

This claims to be the first Spanish language podcast in the USA and is made by Los Blogueros in Washington, DC. El Bloguipodio sets out to give the Latino perspective on world, national and local news, including opinion, commentary, interviews, soundseeing tours, music and entertainment. Given that Spanish is fast taking over in parts of the USA, this is worth tuning in to for a taco-side take on the States.

http://feeds.feedburner.com/ElBloguipodio

phatBrotkasten Inc.

There are more than a hundred episodes already from these podcasters from Bonn, Germany, on subjects as broad ranging as music, literature, sexuality, religion and local events in Bonn. Unstoppable.

www.brotkasten.phatcafer.de/

Das Literatur-Café

The Literature-Café is Wolfgang Tischer's German website for authors and readers. It features tips, interviews, reports, short stories, poems and reviews.

www.literaturcafe.de/feed/podcast.xml

audibleblog.de

It's not all literature in Germany, so to get your regular feed of German language news and entertainment try audibleblog.

www.audibleblog.de/

Here's an idea for you

'Es diferente. Es bonito. Es muy chido. Es Ritmo Latino.' Yes, Ritmo Latino will help you practise your Spanish but more than that it will get your hips shimmying as you do so. Ritmo Latino boasts salsa (of course) but also lesser-known Latin rhythms such as bachata, cumbia, samba, alternative, and electronica. Better than any of these, however, is the one you just have to love, even if you wouldn't take it home to meet mum – the gloriously named 'disco-smut'.

www.ritmolatino.com/

26

Britcasting

Brit podcasting sites

While a bizarre number of podcasts do seem to come from American states dominated by vowels (Idaho, Utah, Indiana, etc.), there are growing numbers of proud podders flying the flag for Britain.

Defining idea

'As always, the British especially shudder at the latest American vulgarity, and then they embrace it with enthusiasm two years later.'
ALISTAIR COOKE (We're getting quicker Alistair.)

Britcaster.com

Easiest of all starting places is inevitably Britcaster.com, the hub for UK podcasts. Originality and creativity are promoted as the hallmarks of Britcast content. Something to do with a quirky national sense of humour and weather that gives us plenty of time indoors with very little else to do makes us naturals at this podcasting lark.

www.britcaster.com

Richard Vobes Radio Show

Richard Vobes is an entertainer and public speaker who has very professionally adapted his skills to producing a daily 30-minute podcast. It's one of the best, as endorsed by the BBC no less. Assisted by his daughter Georgie and friend Jimmy, he delivers entertainment, humour and music, presented with an eccentric British feel and a very un-British lack of amateurism and cock-ups.

www.vobes.com

((URY)) Monday Breakfast

'Two presenters, one baldy, no talent!' No idea what's with the absurd number of brackets either but given that the point of the show is about Matt and Mark 'taking imbecility to new heights' it seems a bit churlish to ask.

http://ury.york.ac.uk/microsite/mattandmark/podcast.rss

Black Country Podcasting

Not sure where the Black Country is? Don't bother looking for it on a map because there's no official area of that name, just a region rich in culture, traditions and dialect as documented here.

www.blackcountrypodcasting.com/

The Urban Sofa Beat Collective

Definitely not life in the countryside. Life in Ipswich, actually, billed as 'Bohemian Internet radio for the culturally diverse'. The Urban

Sofa is a series of 'mumblings' for chaps who like nosh and still aren't sure about Johnny Foreigner (and who can blame them?).

www.theurbansofa.co.uk/rss/urban.xml

Chiltern Heights

Life in the countryside. Something to keep you going while the BBC sorts out the rights to podcast *The Archers*:

http://feeds.feedburner.com/chiltern-heights

The Definitive London Podcast

A title just gagging to be challenged but for now it stands the test with lots of detailed info for those thinking of visiting or even moving to the city.

http://thomed.audioblog.com/rss/definitivelondon.xml

Here's an idea for you

Remember those multi-packs of breakfast cereal that brought you taster-sized mini-boxes of all the family favourites? Well that's what Britpack is ... only without the added sugar and B vitamins. A standard Britpack (there have already been a number of editions) includes up to a baker's dozen (that's thirteen for non-Brits) different podcast samples by British podcasters, ranging from Podcast Paul to the Urban Sofa Beat Collective by way of A Brit Abroad, Slam Idle and the Tartan Podcast. Try this great way to check out a whole load of podcasts.

http://britcaster.com/podcasts/the-britpack-podcast/rss2

Podcast killed the radio star

Commercial radio

Sages have been solemnly proclaiming the death of radio pretty much since the birth of radio. However, despite the usual predictions about podcasting and prime time, commercial radio looks set to embrace podcasting as another string to its bow, or modulation to its frequency.

Defining idea

'TV gives everyone an image, but radio gives birth to a million images in a million brains.'
PEGGY NOONAN, US writer touching on why radio just doesn't seem to want to go away.

In January 2005, a survey for *Billboard* magazine showed that people who listen to mp3 players, internet radio or satellite radio still tune to terrestrial radio two hours and 33 minutes a day, which makes you wonder where they get the time but it doesn't exactly spell death for radio. Indeed the mainstream stations are sniffing cautiously around the podcast phenomenon as a means of extending their reach into the iPod generation. Some also see it as a means of generating extra revenue, such as the move by US talk-show host Rush Limbaugh to offer podcasts of his shows for $50 a year. He's not the only one.

KFMB-FM/100.7 Jack

The snappily-named KFMB-FM/100.7 Jack in San Diego is testing pay-as-you-go with a $5 per month fee for downloading its top-rated morning show. The 'jack' reference, incidentally, refers to a style of radio in which DJ's are dispensed with and music is simply put on an automatic rotation – commonly described as an 'iPod on shuffle'. Radio immitating podlife?

www.sandiegojack.com

BBC Radio 1's Chris Moyles show

Those who prefer to be soothed into wakefulness with the sound of humanity at eyelid-unsticking time will be glad to know that Radio 1's Chris Moyles has joined the poderati and his breakfast show can be downloaded and listened to even if you happened to sleep right through the morning and no longer have a job to go to.

www.bbc.co.uk/radio1/chrismoyles/

Radio Memories

If radio is your thing then how about a bit of pure nostalgia with the prolific Dennis Humphrey, who has put together a seemingly endless string of programmes about the history of radio and the best radio programmes of days gone by. It's a US show although many of the stars such as multi-voiced Mel Blanc will be known to any cartoon fan around the world.

http:/radiomemories.libsyn.com/

Here's an idea for you

Virgin on the ridiculous, Pete and Geoff's Virgin Radio breakfast show, (briefly) made the pod headlines by becoming the first UK radio show to offer a daily podcast (the others just offer highlights during the week). Try it and you can listen to the show every day on the way to work, even if the way to work happens to involve travelling in a metal tube two hundred metres underground. 'Think of it as Sky+ for the Internet, except in your pocket, and nothing to do with telly,' says Virgin, slightly less than helpfully.

www.virginradio.co.uk/breakfast/

28

Heroes

Personal podcasts from the greats

Hero worship takes many forms and a glance at the podcasting listings shows that different people have some very different ideas about who they look up to and want to learn more about. The following is a smorgasbord of stargazing.

Listen with Lance

Hearing heroes themselves is still relatively rare in the podcast panorama but cycling legend Lance Armstrong is an exception. Go to Learn Out Loud and look down the extensive audio and visual offerings for the Texan cycling maestro and you will find a link to Sirius radio's Lance In France series of podcasts. (You can get it at www.sirius.com too, but you'll have to search for it.) What you'll find is a stage by stage report on Lance's record-shattering seventh Tour de France, with input from the man himself. If you look around the Learn Out Loud site you'll also find digital audio on some of his other achievements, including the Livestrong anti-cancer charity that spawned the rash of charity bracelets now gracing wrists everywhere.

www.learnoutloud.com/lancearmstrong

Frat Pack Podcast

There will be Hollywood tribute shows for as long as Tinseltown manages to sparkle but it's often a surprise what tribute makers choose to dedicate themselves to. This is a fairly select weekly podcast because it single-mindedly focuses on the Frat Pack currently dominating US fluffy comedy films (Ben Stiller, Vince Vaughn, Will Ferrell, and Owen and Luke Wilson). On second thoughts, not that single-mindedly because it also looks around for others to include (Jack Black, for example).

www.the-frat-pack.com/the-frat-pack.xml

The Hollywood Podcast

What's different about The Hollywood Podcast is that it is produced by LA actor and writer Tim Coyne and so is coloured by aspirations to be part of the whole star system. Listen in as Coyne interviews fellow Hollywood aspirants and pitches his own ideas for shows to the great and the good in TV and film.

http://hollywoodpodcast.libsyn.com/rss

My Marilyn

Forty years on and there are still those for whom Marilyn Monroe is some kind of beacon. This podcast is for hard-core Marilyn fans with an interest in Marilyn collectibles and the capacity to listen to debate fired up by such earth-shattering revelations as Liz Hurley's comment that Marilyn was fat.

http://feeds.feedburner.com/MyMarilynPodcast

Here's an idea for you

Not all heroes are human, and for the guys at the Golden Age of Comic Books a true hero can easily be spotted by his cape and superpowers. The 'Golden Age' is roughly defined as lasting from 1938 to 1956, a period when the (usually) unspoken backdrop to the cartoon action went from the depression, to World War, and then to the Cold War. Superman, Batman, Captain America and even Donald Duck were all part of the culture of their times and it's that popular culture that Golden Age looks to explore.

www.goldenagecomics.org/

29

Blog podcasting

Soliloquies and rants from around the world

Podcasting started out with blogging (online diaries), and a lot of the better podcasts are still one person's outlook on the world, whether it's from far afield or close to home.

Defining idea

'I never travel without my diary. One should always have something sensational to read in the train.'
OSCAR WILDE

The Daily Source Code

Adam Curry's show, The Daily Source Code, is often cited as the first ever podcast back in the days when software developers made up half of the audience, hence its tagline 'where developers and users party together'. The Daily Source Code mixes technology, the latest developments in podcasting itself and commentary on all things poddy by the podfather himself. For those who produce their own podcasts it's considered to be a bit of an industry bible.

www.dailysourcecode.com/

Morning Coffee Notes

Having celebrated Adam Curry, it's unthinkable not to include Dave Winer because he created RSS, which is the technology behind the podcast subscription system. More laid-back and mellow than The Daily Source Code, but oddly hypnotic, Dave's blog, Morning Coffee Notes, can be found at:

www.morningcoffeenotes.com/

Herro Flom Japan

Rich Pav, the evil mastermind behind Herro Flom Japan, takes the tech and chit-chat formula to another level by combining it with his observations on living in Japan. Rich doesn't have any claims to being the first, the best, the most authoritative – in fact he doesn't claim anything – his podcasts instead being a more stream of consciousness, usually preceded by the term 'I feel a podcast coming on'. Or, as he puts it: 'My bunions are tingling. Every time that happens, a podcast spews forth from deep inside me. Kinda like that movie Alien.' The latest development is the addition of a video feed called The Herro Flom Japan Video Clip Chumbucket, which he admits isn't really good enough to send out, 'but at the same time it's a shame to just throw it away'. Offbeat, oft understated, and often funny.

www.herroflomjapan.com/
video: http:/feeds.feedburner.com/hfj_videochum

Fox and the City

A bit of a different blog this, not least because it doesn't touch on technology much and instead likes to poke fun at celebrities as Ragan Fox takes us in tow on his 'queer comedy' romp. Pretty much anything is up for grabs (though the camper the better) in Ragan's rantings, including politics and fashion, and there are interviews with the creator of the Terry Schiavo Vegetable Diet. Not for the faint hearted.

http://foxinthecity.libsyn.com/

Here's an idea for you

Geek shall always speak unto geek via podcasting – it's their natural medium – but Mur Lafferty's Geek Fu Action Grip is such a class act that it manages to keep geekdom happy (this is a woman who truly understands what's going on in Babylon 5) while also being funny, sarcastic and a lot sharper than your average blogger. But then as she herself points out, she is 'a gamer, a mommy, a writer and a geek all rolled into one'. There are geeks across the Internet with monstrous crushes on this woman, just on the basis of the podcast. Give her a whirl and find out why.

http://essentialmath.com/geekfu/wp-rss2.php

30

I wandered lonely as a pod

Poetry podcasting

While few podcasters can truly be said to wax lyrical, there is a small but dedicated group who feel that ums, ahs, and swearing are only artistically justified if they rhyme. It's time to meet the pod poets.

Defining idea

'Any healthy man can go without food for two days – but not without poetry.'
CHARLES BAUDELAIRE, French poet

PodPoet

A weekly fix of poems can be scored from the PodPoet of San Diego, with occasional guests stopping by to chip in a word or two. PodPoet opts for a simple, even naïve style of poetry, often based on observations of daily life in the US. It's the sort of thing you might listen to in the car on the way to the supermarket rather than save up for moments of inspired introspection locked up in your ivory tower. A poem a week: 'personal, political, powerful, pointless'.

http://podpoet.com
http://feeds.feedburner.com/rizzn/ZljJ

Howl – Allen Ginsberg

Beat poet meets pod in this reading of Allen Ginsberg's Howl set to music.

www.chrisbrauer.com/howl_podcast_cbmp.rss

Poem Present

Not necessarily as fresh and radical as some of the podcast offerings but with a more consistent quality level, the Poem Present podcasts feature modern poetry as filtered through the critical judgement of the University of Chicago. Poem Present was originally a series of lectures and poetry readings from the University of Chicago which someone had the (very) bright idea of recording and making available for podcasters.

http://poempresent.uchicago.edu/poempresent_audio.rss

Sundown Lounge

Not exclusively poetry by any means, this is a podzine mixing a smorgasbord of snippets of poetry, politics, technology and West Coast musings.

www.larrywinfield.com/sundown.xml

SurrealWords.com

A community of contemporary poets who perform live at poetry venues. Originally podcast as a long show, this now comes out in a more easily digested form as the twenty-minute 3rd Eye Pause for Poetry show as well. Be warned that the site host, Empress of Words, is the first to admit that contributors represent 'all skill levels, from hobbyist poet to semi-professionals'.

www.surrealwords.com
http://feeds.feedburner.com/poets-spoken

BadPoetryinMotion

It's not always clear whether BadPoetryinMotion (BPiM to initiates) is named in a refreshingly frank admission of weakness or a spirit of bad-to-the-bone bravado. One current show, In The Raw With Monte Smith, is dedicated to the 'revolutionary spoken word community', which seems to mean modern poets with a flavour of the rap generation and an eye to Che Guevara politics. 'Join the Revolution', exhorts BPiM. Right on, brother.

http://badpoetryinmotion.com

Here's an idea for you

If you're a fan of poetry, investigate the Griffin Trust, a Canadian poetry prize for English language poetry worldwide. It was launched by such luminaries as Margaret Atwood and Michael Ondaatje with the aim of encouraging excellence in poetry. To spread the word about the prize and publicise some of the poetry submitted for it, the organisers have created a podcast directory with samples of the winners and contestants, which makes for something of a *Reader's Digest* shortcut to the innovative and exotic poetry of the moment.

www.griffinpoetryprize.com/podcast/index.html

31

Wayne's World

Amateur 'radio' casts

Podcasting is so simple any idiot can make shows. The problem is that most of them have and finding the truly good pod radio in amongst the endless hours of teenage rant and middle-age self-indulgence can seem like a full-time job. So don't waste your life: just keep an eye on the top ten lists in the main pod portals and while waiting for the latest hot tip to turn up why don't you see if any of the following tickle your fancy?

Jawbone Radio

Ever wondered what life would be like if you had five kids and lived in Cleveland? You sick puppy, you. Well, thankfully you can save yourself the effort of doing it for real and instead tune into the musings and humour of Len and Nora Peralta (as soon as they've put the kids to bed of course). Worth it for the show titles alone ('Guess I'll go and eat a worm', 'I lost my frog', 'That 70's chick'), Jawbone has been compared to Seinfeld in that it's funny yet not actually about anything and, as you might expect from a family in Ohio, it doesn't rely on random swearing for its effect (which is rarer than you'd think in podcasting).

www.jawboneradio.blogspot.com

The Bitterest Pill

A nicely combined mix of comment, nostalgic radio adds from days of yore (love the jingles for smoking) and occasional input from Dan Klass and his daughter (aah) makes for light-hearted easy listening.

www.danklass.com/pill/

The Dawn and Drew Show

Dawn Miceli and Drew Domkus ad lib, banter and badmouth their way through one of the most popular podcasts on the web and certainly one of the more slickly put together. Anyone who has ever listened to the Derek and Clive dialogues (Peter Cook and Dudley Moore) will grumble that it's tame stuff but then again they'll also tell you that policeman look young these days and it was once all trees round here.

www.dawnanddrew.com

Here's an idea for you

To get an idea of where a lot these things started off you should take a sip of Dave Winer's Morning Coffee Notes. One of the very first podcasts, 'what it lacks in production values it makes up for with originality' goes the bumf. Actually, the production values are precisely what you'd expect from one man and his microphone, with the twist that sometimes the man seems to have forgotten that the mike is on. Expect slurping, chewing, rambling and occasional insights on anything from software to where you put your glasses when swimming in the ocean. Despite the total absence of jingles or background music, the happy marriage of a meandering mind and a curiously lyrical delivery makes Dave Winer's laid-back monologues decidedly hypnotic. Truly this man is the Dude of Pod.

www.morningcoffeenotes.com/rss.xml

32
London calling
The BBC and podcasting

With so much *Wayne's World* amateurism on the web it comes as a surprise to find the BBC, that Grand Old Dame of broadcasting, is one of the pioneers. A pleasant surprise, too, judging by the popularity of its podcasts.

Defining idea

'We are taking the phenomenon seriously, not necessarily because of what it does now, but because of what it might allow to become possible later.'
CHRIS BERTHOUD on podcasting.

In amongst the amateur bloggers and the endless Bill and Ted twosomes telling each other knob jokes, the BBC stands out like a dowager duchess at a rave. She can shake her funky stuff too judging by the popularity of the BBC radio programmes, whether they be film reviews or Melvyn Bragg, patron saint of British arts, talking about the life and times of Karl Marx.

So where's our daily dose of the nation's favourite radio show, *The Archers*, then? Chris Berthoud, the man in charge of podcasting, explains what we will and what we won't hear from Auntie Beeb. 'At the moment, we are offering twenty programmes in the download trial from across all of BBC Radio, including the World Service. The programmes have been selected for their range, but also because of their rights status. When it comes to comedy, drama, quizzes and music programmes, we are unable to even think about offering them as downloads. There are some very clever and very high up people in the BBC thinking about the corporation's future in this regard. There are all sorts of implications, not least financial. For example, if we wanted to offer *The Archers* as downloads, deals would have to be struck with the talent unions as well as the writers and actors. And who would pay? Is it an acceptable use of the licence fee? Should people downloading these things abroad be able to access them for free?'

The BBC isn't releasing figures, but Berthoud acknowledges that there are thousands of downloads per week for each of the shows on offer and that 'downloading is not narrowing down people's radio listening, it's in fact encouraging them to try out new shows. Podcasting is exciting for the radio industry. It won't destroy traditional listening, but it opens up yet another way of accessing the great programmes that, for example, Radio 4 produces. There is now even less excuse for missing one.'

The rights issue will remain a headache for broadcasters of drama and comedy, but given the unique way that the BBC is funded, with no dependency on advertising for revenue and a remit to extend its reach to wider audiences, it would be surprising if we didn't see a whole load more quality listening being made available for the pod people.

Here's an idea for you

The trial isn't going to last indefinitely but, while it's still in place, check out the trial site at *www.bbc.co.uk/radio/downloadtrial/*. It provides a one-stop site for all of the twenty shows from the BBC, ranging from the Going Digital technology magazine to Gaelic programming by way of Sportsweek and From Our Own Correspondent. Although not strictly speaking podcasts, there is also a wealth of dowloadable and streaming radio from the main radio site at *www.bbc.co.uk/radio/* from which future podcasts are likely to come.

33

Podcasting down under

For the moment, mainstream podcasting is still largely an English-language affair but that doesn't mean it's just the US and UK voices making themselves heard. Antipodean podcasting is alive and thriving.

G'Day World

Yup they have geeks down under too, and for all things Antipodean and techy you can do a lot worse than G'Day World – 'bring on the podcast . . . you little ripper,' announces the site as it ploughs a furrow through the Linux/Microsoft debates in the land of *Neighbours*.

Defining idea

'I was the toast of two continents: Greenland and Australia.'
DOROTHY PARKER on global success.

www.gdayworld.com/podcast/

Triple J's Hack

All part of the Australian Broadcasting Corporation network, Triple J is Australia's non-commercial radio network for young people and Hack is a half-hour current affairs program covering world politics, social issues, health and the environment.

www.abc.net.au/triplej/hack/

Andy Grace

Andy Grace, I am told, is a legend in the commercial radio space. The catch is that he's a legend in the commercial radio space on the other side of the planet from the one I inhabit, which makes him just another podjock from my perspective. This fifteen-minute daily show is intended to be a chance for him to say things that you won't hear on air. Knockabout topical stuff.

http:/andygrace.com/

Bubble and Squeak

For those not in the know, bubble and squeak is a dish made by reheating old mixed leftovers. This gives you an idea of what the show is all about. Once a week your host, Kez de Clouet, serves up a half hour of geekery, gadgetry, phone fun, funky music, interviews and opinion on everything you never thought was happening in Sydney. It's not the most sophisticated of shows (well, what do you expect from leftovers?) and when in doubt it falls back on naughty words and toilet humour. Nevertheless, it's a bright and bubbly show from modern urban Aussies without corks in their hats.

www.bubbleandsqueakshow.com/

Maynard's Malaise

Of course there has to be at least one Oz show featuring a cobber wandering around chortling at rudeness, and that seems to be Maynard's job in life. Whether it's a romp around the Sydney Sexpo ('remember, it's not a perve-fest, it's a lifestyle expo') or the Mardi Gras Parade ('messy') then Maynard, a veteran of such radio as ABC, is the man to bring it to you.

www.maynard.com.au/downloads/podcast/MaynardsMalaise.xml

Rumpus Room

Music and chatter from Adelaide, South Australia, which brings you the world of tomorrow from the heart of the Green City. Topics include Aussie politicians and their ongoing relationship with the media, sports and the best indie Oz and Kiwi bands.

feed: http://www.osterby.com/portals/8/rss.xml

Here's an idea for you

If you're not an Aussie and you haven't made the trip, surprise yourself by learning just how much modern Australia looks towards Asia. Amongst the media big boys down under, SBS is a good start for a general exploration of the multi-culturalism that is modern Oz. World View is a series of podcasts looking at such issues as commercial lychee farming, sunken treasure, African hip hop in Oz, and the role of Vietnamese refugees in society.

www20.sbs.com.au/podcasting/
feed: http:/feeds.feedburner.com/sbs_worldview

34
Local life
Local news and community casting

Because podcasts can be pretty much free to create and distribute, they lower the barriers to broadcasting and make it available to a lot of small communities that wouldn't otherwise have a voice. Tune in to some of the local life on planet podcast and you may find yourself thinking about creating one of your own.

Defining idea

'There's nineteen men livin' in my neighborhood / Eighteen of them are fools / and the one ain't no doggone good.'
BESSIE SMITH, blues singer, and a perfect example of compelling local reporting.

Charlottesville Podcasting Network

CPN is a useful lesson on the fact that local doesn't have to mean lacking in outlook. Evidently proud of the Central Virginia region and the home of Thomas Jefferson, CPN also offers documentary and talk on 'everything from Nietzsche to road-building, comic books to global security'.

www.cvillepodcast.com/wp-rss2.php

114

StandardNETCAST

Here are daily stories from the top of Utah, including the pulsing heart of the Weber/Davis metro area, and more. If you want to hear about developments at the Treehouse Museum or downtown's Ogden Brewski then who else you gonna call?

www.standard.net/pods/index.php

Bath Chinese Broadcasting

This one's particularly unusual because of being a community within a community. Bath is a long way west of the bamboo curtain and yet BCB hopes to bring Chinese culture to the local community. It's the brainchild of the University of Bath Chinese Student Society and just goes to show that not all students spend their student years permanently drunk.

http://radio.bathchisoc.com/home/

Warner Alliance Church

There are more church community podcasts than you can shake a surplice at, and this is a reasonable example of one from your friendly Lewiston Idaho community, including online Sunday sermons.

www.warneralliance.com/

N.E. Derbyshire Community Radio

One of the first licensed 'Community Radio Stations' in the UK, N.E. Derbyshire is a not-for-profit community radio aimed at both educating would-be broadcasters and helping the community. It features talks on alternative medicine, fitness and issues of interest to the elderly.

www.regencyradio.com/

Community Affairs

This show is interesting not because it is a local community show (it isn't) but because it's about helping local community and non-profit making organisations to get their messages across even with the limited resources available to them. The podcast is simply a part of practising what they preach in that respect.

website: www.communityaffairs-usa.com
feed: http:/bmmedia.podblaze.com/skin_bmmedia.xml

Here's an idea for you

Every now and again you come across a local radio podcast that you suspect is being beamed in from another planet. Nimbinradiomedia is one of those. Nimbin is an alternative lifestyle village in Australia where hippies are still the latest news and drug law reform is perhaps the most pressing political issue since anyone could actually remember another one. Tune in to find out about Naked Hippy Jack and how the Chickens of Collateral are going to repay the English in full for sins of yesteryear. Or something.

http:/nimbinradiomedia.libsyn.com/rss

35
Talking books

If you miss being tenderly tucked in at night with a story at bedtime then why not get your mp3 player to do the job for you? Talking books make perfect portable audio.

Defining idea

'Books are more than books. They are the life, the very heart and core of ages past, the reason why men lived and worked and died, the essence and quintessence of their lives.'
AMY LOWELL, US poet and critic

Podumentary, my dear Watson

Sherlock Holmes is popular worldwide and tends to break down into perfectly podable bite-size pieces for podcasting so it comes as no surprise to find that no fewer than five of his adventures are available. *A Study in Scarlet, The Adventures of Sherlock Holmes, The Memoirs of Sherlock Holmes, The Return of Sherlock Holmes* and *The Sign of Four* can all be found at Pink Geek Audio.

www.pinkgeekaudio.net/weblog3/

Stories To Go

Short stories are a natural for the mp3 format because they are quick to download, don't take up too much space on portable players, and are about the right run time to transport you to another plane while the bus/tram/subway transports you to work. Stories To Go mixes up classic and modern short stories to download, bringing together a fascinating blend of authors you probably have heard of (Edgar Allen Poe, William Carlos Williams) and those you probably haven't (James Branch Cabell, Einar H. Kvaran).

http://storiestogo.blogspot.com/

KCRW 'Bookworm'

This is not strictly speaking a talking book but instead a podcast literary magazine showcasing fiction and poetry by new, emerging and established authors, usually in the form of interviews by the host, Michael Silverblatt. It's ideal for those for whom simply reading books is not enough.

www.kcrw.org/show/bw

Shakespeare By Another Name

Shakespeare By Another Name is a book by Mark Anderson (with notes from renowned actor Derek Jacobi) about the true identity of the Bard of Avon. Nothing too unusual there – Shakespeare has been variously identified as everyone from Bacon to Jack the Ripper – but where Anderson is breaking new ground is in using podcasting to provide excerpts to help market the book; something I suspect we are going to see (hear?) a lot more of in the future.

http:/shakespearebyanothername.com/audio.html

Here's an idea for you

It may go against the grain to pay for a podcast but Audible is encouraging you to do just that. Audible is well established in the States as an online bookshop for talking books as well as radio drama and audio magazines. The idea is that for a fixed fee per month (currently £9.49/$17.17) you can download all you like and there are no limitations on the number of times you listen to what you've got (not always the case with other services). The site talks the talk with a host of audio samples to check out and it's worth a visit to stream the Eddie Izzard *Glorious* audio sample if nothing else.

www.audible.co.uk

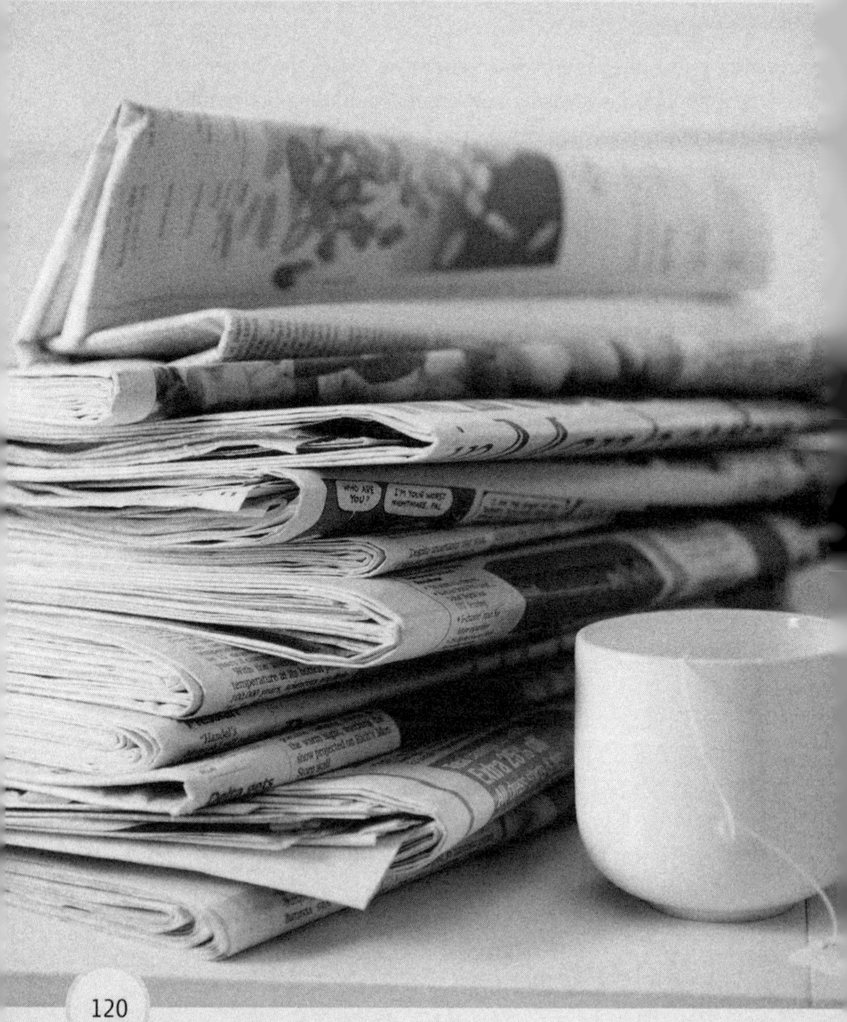

36

Talking newspapers

Newspapers too are trying to find ways in which they and their readerships can benefit from podcasting, a puzzle to which they seem to have come up with a surprising variety of answers. Whether it's audio news or magazine programmes based around newspaper sections, the papers are working on all manner of ways to add audio to their output. Here are just a few of them.

Defining idea

'A newspaper is not just for reporting the news as it is, but to make people mad enough to do something about it.'
MARK TWAIN

The sharp eyed will spot that, to date, these examples are all US-based newspapers. The rest of the world is still waiting before somebody else will 'read all about it' out loud to us.

Denverpost.com Podcast Central

The *Denver Post* is one of the first newspapers to offer a daily audio edition aimed at commuters. It features a full eight-minute version or, if you prefer, just the sections on business, local, national or sports news. The paper uses journalism students to record the items to their own computers in the middle of the night – cunning, cutting edge … and cheap.

www.denverpost.com/podcasts

San Francisco Chronicle

After a tentative start, the SFC seems to have launched enthusiastically into podcasting with a rotating school of journalists discussing news, food and Arnold Schwarzenegger (well, he is their governor). The news behind the news.

http://sfchroniclebiz.blogspot.com/

Ventura County Star

This covers local news stories with interviews of the reporters, editors, columnists and others. You'll also get a song a day of (mostly) local music, plus a weekend show for lots of music and much less talk.

http://feeds.feedburner.com/VenturacountystarcomPodcast

Monroe Evening News

Daniel J. Eizans, the entertainment writer, has his own podcast covering just about anything from reality TV to music and the latest CDs.

www.monroenews.com/columnists/daniel_eizans-community/

GameOn

Similarly, the *Columbus Dispatch* – 'Ohio's Greatest Newspaper' – has given a podcast to its gaming section, GameOn! with Shawn Sines and Chuck Nelson. As well as recording audio reviews of games, this gives the guys a chance to go and talk to gaming champions and developers about their passion.

www.dispatch.com/gameon

Seattle Post Intelligencer

Another area that newspapers are looking at for the podcast format is the food section so beloved of magazines (and traditional broadcasting). For a taste of things to come in that direction, try the *Seattle Post Intelligencer*'s food editor, who has her own podcast called On Food with Hsiao-Ching Chou.

http://seattlepi.nwsource.com/podcast/onfood.asp

Here's an idea for you

You can get an interesting flavour of the diversity of what the papers are offering from the *Philadelphia Daily News*. Its Philly Feed takes a different approach: the hosts' goal is to offer people information they don't get in the printed edition. Why? Well, because, as Frank Burgos, the page editor of the *Philadelphia Daily News*, puts it, 'having someone read me the news isn't as entertaining as it may seem'. Instead, Burgos and Mayberry (the advertising director) interview other writers about stories to get more depth or 'colour', play a little music, and chit chat about sports. On a more serious note, they also invite serious prize-winning journalists into the studio and give them the chance to express more about their stories than can be told in a thousand words of newsprint.

www.phillyfeed.com/

37

Arnie goes audio

Podcast politics

Politicians are pod people too, or so their spin doctors would like us to think, and inevitably when presented with any means of reaching an audience it'll be the candidates who reach for the microphones.

Defining idea

'I adore political parties. They are the only place left to us where people don't talk politics.'
OSCAR WILDE

Bob Dole

In the US, both Democrats and Republicans are beating a path to podcasting in the hope of getting their say. Former presidential candidate Bob Dole is using podcasting (available via the official Republican party site), although he seems more interested in promoting his 'One Soldier's Story' than his party.

www.rnc.org

Senator Edwards

Meanwhile, Senator Edwards and his wife Elizabeth have their own half-hour broadcasts in which the Edwards chat politics and answer questions sent in by visitors to the website. They don't bother with the rude ones, by the way, so don't bother – I've tried.

www.oneamericacommittee.com

Republican Radio

Party political radio strikes me as more than a little odd but if you are the kind of person who enjoys nothing better than tuning in to 'the standard bearer of the Conservative movement in San Francisco' then you'll have a ball with Republican Radio and its bright, shiny new podcast.

www.republicanradio.com/

Audio Activism

At the other end of the scale there is the politics of the street with the likes of Audio Activism, which features audio recorded at political rallies and in the street itself. Be warned that the quality of that comment does tend to vary: one suspects that 'Brandon's' bold dismissal of the last Gulf War as 'not really cool, you know' may not actually do much to reshape the planet. It's more fun than the polished politico poddery, though.

www.audioactivism.org

British politics

With the major parties (party?) and their budgets tying up most of the airtime available on mainstream media, it is logical to find that the Liberal Democrats were the first to turn to podcasting. Charles Kennedy's campaign to right the wrongs of British politics, and perhaps wipe the grin off Blair's face, can be found at:

www.kennedycampaign.org/

Election fever

This is one that will be fun to tuck away for a rainy day, or more specifically for the next general election. The Election podcast brings together quotes from the election speeches of British politicians, thereby providing a handy and amusing way of seeing who delivers on promises, and indeed who bothers to write a new speech next time around. The podcast feed for this is at:

http:/mp3.phoneticpodcast.com/uk.xml

Here's an idea for you

Although the original idea of the podcasts was to bring 'the people of California closer in touch with their Governor', the appeal of this site is universal when you remember that the governor in question is Arnold Schwarzenegger. Yep, the man most famous for playing a homicidal robot from the future has a weekly podcast so that you too can pretend to listen to his political agenda while actually just enjoying his accent and picturing him discussing health benefits while strapping weapons all over his body. The podcast feed is:

http:/features.governor.ca.gov/index.php/podcast/rss/

38

Podcasters for the people

Voices from troubled nations

Podcasting doesn't require expensive equipment and it is very hard for a government to control so one of the burgeoning areas of broadcasting covers subjects from states that would normally mute or suppress the message. Whether from Tibet or Iran, podcasts allow you to hear what the politicians would rather you didn't.

Defining idea

'The less people know about what is really going on, the easier it is to wield power and authority.'
PRINCE OF WALES, (not an elected position the last time we checked).

Mr Behi Blogs

Iran is a country where getting impartial local information is a little tricky and so we can be thankful for the tireless Mr Behi who blogs regularly from Iran. His themes include Iranian politics and the US rumour and criticism thereof, which is a pretty rich vein at the moment as the US and Europe take it in turns talk warily with the new government.

website: http:/mrbehi.blogs.com/
feed: www.feedburner.com/MrBehiBC

Persian podcast

If the above interests you then you may also want to know that the first Persian language programme is also being podcast. The BBC's Rooze Haftom offers an arts and entertainment programme highlighting the decidedly non-official side of culture. Where else are you going to listen to Iranian death metal?

www.bbc.co.uk/persian/
or in English, try the BBC podcasting page at:
www.bbc.co.uk/radio/downloadtrial/

Epoch Times on China

As the followers of the Dalai Lama will doubtless concur, China is not the freest of countries when it comes to news gathering or commentary. This leaves it down to the likes of podcaster Epoch Times to broadcast its 'Nine Commentaries on the Chinese Communist Party', a critique of the Chinese Communist Party (CCP). You do have to wonder if the Epoch Times isn't being just a little premature, however, in aiming to 'pass a final judgement before the lid is laid on the coffin of the Communist Party'.

website: http:/english.epochtimes.com/jiuping.asp
feed: www.sohpodcast.com/jiuping.xml

Zimbabwe

Although currently soft-pedalling on the politics (for fear of reprisals), there is now a Shona language podcast about life, language and food (you're never far from food in podcasting) by an Anglo-Zimbabwean couple.

www.shonapodcast.co.uk

Singapore RadioSDP

At time of writing the Singapore Democratic Party has announced RadioSDP as the first political podcast from Singapore. It is described as a way for the party to bypass Singapore's state-controlled media. The podcast hasn't actually hit the air yet but it is promised in four languages (English, Chinese, Malay, and Tamil). The party asks Internet users to play the podcast 'to the older generation of Singaporeans, such as your parents and grandparents, who may not have the necessary computer and literacy skills to read our website'.

www.singaporedemocrat.org

Here's an idea for you

Catch a real winner for LamRim, Tibetan Buddhist Internet Radio, in the form of a genuine global A-list broadcaster – the Dalai Lama uses the platform to present such wisdom as the 'Heart Sutra', 'Lamp for the Path of Enlightenment' and the 'Path of Liberation Teachings'. Totally and utterly in his shadow, there are also numerous other teachers who get to give their version of the tantric grounds and paths but it really must be a bit like being a backing singer to Madonna.

website: www.lamrim.com
feed: www.lamrim.com/podcasts/rss.php

39

In Pod we trust

Godcasting

Religion is one of the most talked about subjects on earth and, unsurprisingly, one of the most podcasted in the podosphere. Christianity tends to dominate (Islam, for example, is very poorly podded) but here are some very different takes from a world of disparate beliefs.

Defining idea

'**Infidel**, *n. In New York, one who does not believe in the Christian religion; in Constantinople, one who does.'*
AMBROSE BIERCE, The Devil's Dictionary.

The Infidel Guy Show

This controversial call-in radio show discusses philosophy, atheism, theology, the paranormal, science and evolution. Much of its drive is a response to creationists and other fundamentalist Christians.

www.infidelguy.com

Freedom From Religion

A relatively new one this, but fairly promising. The Freedom From Religion podcast is dedicated to exposing how dogmatic religious traditions, adherence to ancient texts that claim to be the answer to every question in life, and rejection of critical examination of ideas puts the future of humanity in jeopardy. Each show features discussion, derision of dogma, and occasional tequila drinking.

http:/lazyacrestudios.libsyn.com/rss

Catholic Mormon Podcast

'Rob is a cradle Catholic and Sarah was born and raised Mormon.' A podcast about the daily tensions, tears, and humour of this couple bringing up a family.

http:/catholicmormon.libsyn.com/rss

Praystation Portable

I couldn't resist this just for the name. Praystation Portable lets you subscribe to the feed and download a daily morning and evening prayer that you can take with you on the road.

http:/feeds.feedburner.com/praystationportable

Catholic Insider

Father Roderick takes you on a journey of discovery through the weird and wonderful world of the Catholic Church. A show filled with music, humour, soundseeing tours, documentaries, interviews and much more.

http://feeds.feedburner.com/catholicinsider

Zencast

Hosted by Amber Star (do you think that's a real name?), this is an introduction to meditation; 'a stream of the living Dharma'.

http://feeds.feedburner.com/Zencast

What is Judaism?

Larry Josephson, a secular Jew who now wants to know more about the religion of his grandparents, asks Rabbi Ismar Schorsch, Chancellor of the Jewish Theological Seminary, to explain the meaning of the Jewish holidays. Interspersed with music, these expand into a pleasant and informal introduction to the religion.

www.whatisajew.org/wij.xml

Rabbi Garfinkel's Podcast

A good deal less informal (and less musical) than the above, Rabbi Garfinkel specialises in weekly commentary on portions of the Torah.

http:/homepage.mac.com/rabbigarfinkel1/podcasts/myfeed.xml

Hindu Podcasting; Devi Mandir Podcasts

I can't honestly claim to know what Shiva Puja is but this is where to find out. Scriptures and Satsang with Shree Maa and Swami Satyananda Saraswati. Super.

http:/feeds.feedburner.com/devnath

Here's an idea for you

You may not agree with the institution but you really can't fault the Vatican when it comes to podcasting. Granted, it does have funds the likes of which the other podcasters can only dream of but that's no reason not to listen in to the Vatican Radio podcasts and admire the slick professionalism from the Holy See.

www.105live.vaticanradio.org/

40

Podding all over the world

Podcast travel guides

Travel guide podcasts range from audio blogs by backpackers to increasingly slick presentations and city guides being created by travel and media companies. Here are a few selected from various points along that spectrum.

Defining idea

'I would like to spend my whole life travelling, if I could borrow another life to spend at home.'
WILLIAM HAZLITT, English essayist making a pretty good case for armchair travel.

Out Here On The Road

Definitely different, this is a podcast from the point of view of the interstate truck driver. Refreshingly free from the 'C'mon now, Good Buddy' stuff, it interviews all sorts of folk making their living driving from one side of the States to the other. The only catch is that diesel mechanics and furniture movers don't always wax lyrical about their lifestyles, but at least they don't all pretend to be some kind of modern cowboy.

http://feeds.feedburner.com/OutHereOnTheRoad

Sushi Radio.com

Sushi Radio is really a cocktail of podcasts from podcasters all over the world, neatly wrapped up and presented (hence the 'sushi' approach) on this site. The kind of material varies wildly from traditional Spanish music (information on sardana, flamenco and rumba Catalana from the British Council in Barcelona) to a night-time walk through the zoo in Singapore or a celebration of old trains in Germany. Very toothsome.

http://sushiradio.com/podcast.php

Josh in Japan

Josh is one of a long and honourable succession of westerners who have made their way to Japan and found themselves stunned by it. The podcast is a weekly attempt to make sense of it for those of us who are not Japanese while the website allows you to send in your own questions for Josh to answer.

website: www.joshinjapan.com/
feed: http://feeds.feedburner.com/JoshInJapan

Notes from Spain

Brits have long hankered after a life in the Spanish sun and this bundle of news, comment and audio tours of the regions prides itself on being 'the first English podcast from one of the greatest countries in Europe'. As such, it also belongs in another fast-growing subculture of the genre, namely expat podcasting, in which those who have made the move paint a realistic picture of what it's like for those still thinking of it.

http:/notesfromspain.libsyn.com/rss

Here's an idea for you

While the backpackergrams and mix-and-match approaches will always throw up surprises, the approach that you are likely to see a lot more of is that of Virgin Atlantic, which has announced a whole series of podcast guides. Virgin is a media company, a radio company and an airline so it all comes together in these guides to eating and visiting cities. (Try the first one out: Virgin Podcasting Guide to New York.) The question is just how long it is before they complete the loop and let travellers download the guides from the in-flight entertainment as they approach their destinations.

http:/virginatlantic.loudish.com/

41
Podcast cuisine

Eating, drinking, podcasting

Food and wine turn out to be right up there with technology and conspiracy in the list of podcaster priorities. Indulge your appetite.

Defining idea

'Cooking is like love. It should be entered into with abandon or not at all.'

HARRIET VAN HORNE, journalist

Winecast

You've already figured out what this one's about, right? In full, enhanced podcast glory (so there are pics too), this site is something of an homage to Zinfandel and Chenin Blanc. An enthusiast's site with something of a citrus nose, interesting herb, green apple and honey flavours, with a dose of acidity and slightly mineral finish.

www.winecast.net/

CoffeeGeek

The site for people who take their coffee so seriously they get unnaturally excited by a shiny espresso machine – though who wouldn't feel the need to lie down for a while when confronted with the likes of a Jura Capresso Impressa S9 Super Automatic dual thermablock machine? Phwoar!

www.coffeegeek.com/

DFW Tequila Tastings

One tequila, two tequila, three tequila, floor.

http://dfw.tequilatastings.com/rsspodcast.xml

Cheers to Wine and Food

A prolific podcast on all things taste-bud-worthy, Linda Bramble offers daily tips on food and wine. Well, to be strictly honest, wine mainly. Not that there's anything wrong with that.

http://cheers.libsyn.com/rss

Pacific Palate

Comfortably padded food journalist Don Genova lives on the Pacific Coast of British Columbia, which suits him just fine because it means he's well placed to talk seafood and wine, often in the company of farmers who share his fascination with ingredients.

www.pacificpalate.com/

Jim's Kitchen

Chef Jim's suggestions go so far as to include sensual menus to 'turn you and your significant other on'. Oddly enough, this doesn't appear to involve liberally coating each other with liquid chocolate. Despite that, Chef James Jondreau turns out a fine mix of recipes, restaurant reviews (rather less useful) and 'an epicurean surprise with each show'.

www.podarama.com/podcasts/chefjondreau/rss.xml

The Podchef Gastrocast

'Gastrocasting' in action, as Neal Foley brings you a show of 'burps, glitches, opinionated facts and spurious cooking tips'. Hell's kitchen, the dangers of cooked rice, recipes and kitchen mayhem in general.

http://feeds.feedburner.com/podchef

Craft Beer Radio

Hosts Jeff Bearer and Greg Weiss (you expected two women, perhaps?) discuss real beer and home-brewing.

www.craftbeerradio.com/

Vegan Cooking School

If you are interested in learning how to cook great vegan dishes, then this is the place for you. Each week Vegan Cooking School publishes a new show that teaches you everything you need to know to incorporate vegan meals into your diet.

www.podsumer.com/vegancookingschool/index.xml

Here's an idea for you

Since the beauty of podcasting is that you decide on just when and where to indulge, it seems to go perfectly with the concept of a happy hour that you yourself declare and exploit. Try out The Real Happy Hour, where you'll find an intense ongoing discussion about the best ingredients for a Bloody Mary, cocktail tips and general happy hour happiness. A new drink is featured each week, meaning happy, nay ecstatic, hours aplenty.

http:/feeds.feedburner.com/TheRealHappyHour

42

Podcast poker

Online poker has taken off like web wildfire, not least because it doesn't penalise those of us whose best attempt at a poker face results in an expression like a warthog chewing a tennis ball. It was just a matter of time before podcasting drew up a stool at the table and threw its hand in on the green baize.

Lord Admiral Radio

A strange name unless you happen to know of the Lord Admiral Card Club in Toronto at which point it all starts to make sense. The Lord Admiral Radio podcast is a weekly offering at the shrine of poker and is hosted by two members of the card club who discuss card playing in casinos and interview the hard-core poker players. It's one for the

Defining idea

'The poker player learns that sometimes both science and common sense are wrong; that the bumblebee can fly; that, perhaps, one should never trust an expert; that there are more things in heaven and earth than are dreamt of by those with an academic bent.'
DAVID MAMET, playwright.

fans of strategy more than atmosphere, since this is the world of serious men sat quietly at small tables with no go-go girls or Elvises in the building at all.

www.lordadmiral.com/radio

Five Hundy by Midnight

If go-go girls and Elvises are what you like along with your royal flush then Five Hundy by Midnight is the original Las Vegas podcast, covering 'all things' Las Vegas, from casino, hotel and restaurant reviews to comps, slot clubs, video poker, blackjack and boozing. From my own hazy memories of the desert resort, that's not strictly true because it spares the tender pod listener a fair number of the 'all things' Las Vegas that verge on the sleaze. One for fans of the atmosphere more than the turn of the cards.

www.fivehundybymidnight.com/fhbm/

Sin City Insider

Another one for Vegas fans, with info for those aiming to visit and in particular the bizarre tips of 'Tim the Taxi Driver'. It's far from being focused on poker but it does cover Las Vegas specials, including the World Series of Poker notes.

www.sincity-insider.com/

Ante Up

Back to the tables for this podcast, which is a bit like being taught to gamble by a couple of reprobate uncles. Ante Up comes from the *Tampa Bay Times* and features host Christopher Cosenza and betting columnist Scott Long as they mull over the finer points of the game and give tips on how to play it better and best of all how not to lose your shirt in the process.

www.tampabay.com/podcasts/feeds/AnteUpPokerCast_rss.xml

Here's an idea for you

For some players, online poker isn't a substitute for the real thing; it is the real thing. Poker Diagram is purely dedicated to the world of online, real time, real money tournament poker so there are no Vegas-style fripperies to get in the way of play. Consequently it is a podcast for the purist, since anyone not completely absorbed by the technicalities of the game is likely to find it 'boring and rather confusing' (in the words of the producer). If, on the other hand, you are looking for description and close analysis of online poker as it happens, 'along with a little idle chat and banter from two clueless Brits ...' then you're definitely in the right place.

www.pokerdiagram.com/

43
Podercise

Pump that podcast

Podcasting has a bit of a split
personality with distinctly couch
potato leanings from its radio side and
a get-out-there-and-do-it aspect from
its portability. These are podcasts from
the dark side, the one where there is no gain without pain.

Defining idea

*'I have never taken any exercise
except sleeping and resting.'*
MARK TWAIN

Marina's Workouts

It's hard to consider podercise without the ever-energetic Marina
popping up somewhere so let's get it over with now shall we?
Marina's Walking Workout Podcast is not, as you might expect,
about ambling around town but actually a High-NRG workout
tailored for speed walkers, step classes, or aerobics.

www.marinaspodcast.com/walking.xml

Marina's Bodysculpting Podcast, on the other hand, is a much slower
beat workout for circuit training or body toning with light weights.
(Nice focus on abs too.)

www.marinaspodcast.com/bodysculpting.xml

Then there are Marina's Musical Workouts, which come without verbal instructions and just leave you to get on with whatever it was you were doing. That's presuming that whatever it was you were doing requires a tempo of 90–150 beats per minute.

www.marinaspodcast.com/noinstruction.xml

By this time you're thinking 'take a break woman, for heaven's sake', at which point, fortunately, she does . . . in the form of Marina's Sitting To The Beat, which is all about exercises you can do while sitting on an airplane, on your couch or in your office chair. Well, it's nice to be able to put your feet up for once.

www.marinaspodcast.com/sitting.xml

Become Your Best Coaching

What makes personal trainers so sure about the regimes they impose? Coach Jeremy Likness interview fitness gurus, trainers and those individuals you see in the 'before and after' pictures to try and get some answers as to what works and what doesn't in the fitness field.

http:/feeds.feedburner.com/BecomeYourBestCoachingPodcast

Running Injury Free

Because there are only two types of runners – the ones who have suffered injury and the ones who are going to suffer injury – everything from shin splints to ligament tears is considered in this podcast. It likes to stress the importance of warm ups, warm downs and stretching to prevent rather than cure.

http:/allen.audioblog.com/rss/runninginjuryfree.xml

TrailCast

Running at lower speeds and with better views is what TrailCast is about. More a hiking podcast than one for trail runners, it's mainly an interview format with hikers, trail associations and equipment manufacturers.

www.trailcast.org/

Here's an idea for you

Great as it is to be goaded along by lycra-clad fanatics, don't you find it can also be motivating to hear tales from other normal beings? Well, 2 Down is a podcast about two thirty-somethings on a quest to shed the pounds and unstick their sorry rear ends from the sofa. They're giving it a go with improved diet and regular exercise to lose weight and get fitter and provide a diet/training partnership for you which promises to be honest about their slip ups just as much as their successes.

http:/2down.podcastplace.com/

44

Queer eye for the pod guy

Fashion

Fashion and technology haven't always sat that comfortably with each other but there's room in podcasting for every flavour, from Geek Chic to Queer Flair and cattiness about all things catwalk.

Defining idea

*'Fashion is what one wears oneself.
What is unfashionable is what other
people wear.'*
OSCAR WILDE

Fashiontribes

An astonishingly rich weekly that podcasts on the subjects of shopping, body dissatisfaction, dressing for your shape, style, shoes, and enough info to keep the girls in *Sex and the City* talking for several more series. There are tips and talk from established fashion authors for anyone (well, anyone female) with even a passing interest in what looks back at you from the mirror and enough in-depth to keep even the Manolo maniacs dribbling.

http:/fashiontribes.typepad.com/main/weekly_fashion_podcast/

Queer Eye for the Straight Guy

Gay men, we are told, are instinctively better dressed and turned out than their straight brethren so who better to spruce up those dull old heteros than a gaggle of uber-slick gents who normally bat for the other side. That's the thinking behind the TV series on both sides of the Atlantic and that's also the thinking behind the weekly Queer Eye podcasts, put out to make the world a smarter and tidier place for all of us. Turn on, tune in and never again wear Speedo, or arrive underdressed for a formal event.

www.bravotv.com/Queer_Eye_for_the_Straight_Guy/Podcasts/

Geek and Chic

Geek chic is still seen as a contradiction in terms for most people and Geek and Chic (the website formerly known as Technosexual) is intended as 'a guide to the Geek in need of style, and the Stylish in need of geek'. This seems to translate to a very geeky lust for gadgets but since few of us are truly immune you may want to listen in and find out more about those to-die-for sunglasses/mp3 players.

www.geekandchic.com

Home Spa Goddess Show

The title says it all really – this is a podcast about the very best in oils, unctions and other slippery things to slap on all over when it's bath time. It features, tips, froth, and more fancy bubble bath than you can throw a rubber duck at.

www.homespagoddess.com

Here's an idea for you

Reject all this fashion nonsense and free yourself from the tyranny of a handful of stick-thin, trust-fund trendies on the fashion mags. Learn why they're not to be trusted at Pop Goes The Culture. PGTC has a pretty wide remit, taking in anything from the world of popular culture. One of its themes (look it up under the May 17, 2005 edition) is that fashion magazines differ from other specialist publications by not hiring employees with any particular expertise in the field, the result being that the glossies reflect a world 'not meant for us ... yet they hold power and sway over teens and make the rest of us feel like fashion failures'. Right on. Throw off your shackles and break out those shell suits with pride.

www.popgoestheculture.com/

45

Escape pod

Escapism and sci-fi

The crossover between the technologically savvy and the sci-fi fan meant that there were always going to be podcasts featuring lasers, time travel and bug-eyed monsters. Take a holiday from your corner of the time/space continuum without leaving the boundaries of your own head.

Defining idea

'Individual science fiction stories may seem as trivial as ever to the blinder critics and philosophers of today – but the core of science fiction, its essence, has become crucial to our salvation if we are to be saved at all.'
ISAAC ASIMOV

Escape Pod

Proudly titled *The SF podcast magazine*, host Stephen Eley does a fair job of living up to the billing with a weekly reading of short stories (science fiction, fantasy, or horror) followed by a discussion of the genre and an invitation to submit your own stories.

http://escape.extraneous.org/podcast.xml

Earth Core

This is the planet's first podcast novel, released in 45-minute episodes every week. A cross between the style of TV show 24 and the subject matter of *Predator* or *Starship Troopers*, *Earth Core* has consistently garnered high downloads and ratings on the podcast portals. Even as it draws to a climax, and with that the inevitable publishing on paper and CD, there are still those who would prefer to podcast the chapters rather than read them off the page.

http://feeds.feedburner.com/earthcore

The Pocket and the Pendant

This is a talking book performance of *ForeWord Magazine*'s 2005 Book of the Year Finalist for SciFi/Fantasy. Our hero, Max Quick, goes from being a bullied 12-year-old to an old-fashioned adventurer when time suddenly stops. In fact the podcast is more than simply an audio book because readings are interspersed with episodes discussing the characters' motivation. While this means that you have to take care (download the wrong podcast and you will hear spoilers about what is going to happen) but it is a brilliant idea. It's like reading a book at the same time as other people and then being able to listen in to conversations about the whys and wherefores of the action to date.

http://feeds.feedburner.com/pocketpendant

Michael and Evo's Dragon Page/Slice of Sci-fi

The Dragon Page is a weekly show about sci-fi, gaming and fantasy (but then you probably guessed that from the title) in which hosts Michael R. Mennenga and Evo Terra chat about comics, technology and huge fire-breathing scaly things. In short it's a dose of random sci-fi geeking out. If you take to Michael and Evo, you'll be happy to know that they also have a show specifically focused on sci-fi in films, TV and music. Called Slice of Sci-fi, it combines chat with interviews featuring both cast and creators.

http://dragonpage.com/podcast.xml
http://feeds.feedburner.com/sliceofscifi

Here's an idea for you

Read the latest Harry Potter already? Getting withdrawal symptoms from Harry, Hagrid, Malfoy, and the Weasleys? Need a further dollop of HP sauce? Well, then try a podcast on the Christian symbolism and biblical references of the Harry Potter books. Father Roderick leads the way on this quest through the hidden meanings and allusions of the world of wizards and warlocks to provide some unexpected insights into his interpretation of muggles, dementors, et al.

http://feeds.feedburner.com/secretsofharrypotter

46

Podcast chic

Playing podcasts through watches, shades, even luggage

The point of podcasts is that they travel with you to be played when and where it tickles your fancy. For some people that also means getting fancy with the playback so here are a few of the latest fashions.

Defining idea

'Art produces ugly things which frequently become beautiful with time. Fashion on the other hand, produces beautiful things which always become ugly with time.'
JEAN COCTEAU

Time to podcast

MP3 watches download music from your computer just like any other music player and then sit on your wrist waiting for you to find time to listen. Until the day they become totally wireless you'll still need a USB cable to download music to them and a pair of headphones to plug into them to listen, but they certainly mean you always have your podcast on your person. Amongst the options for clockwatching podcasts are the BMW version (www.bmw-online.com) for the busy exec, the Aussie version E@Time (www.etimedigtech.com.au/), the Windows only Casio WMP-1V (www.casio.com), or the 'bling attitood' G-Unit (www.g-unitsoldier.com/) from 50 Cent (and if you don't know who he is you probably shouldn't be wearing the watch).

Podcaster baggage?

Remember when portable stereo meant a boom box the size of a fridge lugged around on someone's shoulder? You might have thought that the iPod and micro mp3 players spelt the end of that, but no – Boom Bag has come up with a solution for those who like their players tiny but still want the world to know they're there. Boom Bags are wheelie-suitcases with built-in speakers, amplifier and subwoofer. Wheelie bag chic?

www.viasf.com/boombags/product.html

Chic shades

MP3 players in your sunglasses? You bet. As ever, leading the field in fashion (and price) is Oakley with the Thump (http://oakley.com/thump/), a piece of gloriously high-tech/tribal must-have gadgetry that looks like it came straight out of the *Matrix*. The headphones are built into the arms of the shades and you just pull the buds down to your ears to listen. Actually, the headphones in these things look more like an instrument of torture but they're oh so cool. A cheaper alternative are the Fio MP3 sunglasses from Global American Technologies (www.globalat.com). All this suggests that we may soon be inundated with mp3 shades and, after that, probably mp3 bifocals and hearing aids as geek chic goes granny.

Here's an idea for you

You don't have to take speakers with you if you want to party with your podcasts or play them to an audience. Just take a Soundbug. You plug the Soundbug into your headphone jack and then stick the bug onto any flat surface (windows are very good). It converts the electronic signals into mechanical energy causing the flat surface to vibrate like a sounding board. It's not going to deafen a room or replace hi-fi, but it does mean you've got speakers anywhere there's a desk, window, or mirror.

www.soundbug.biz

47

Rolling your own

Putting together your first podcast

Got a computer? A microphone? Headphones? Something to say? Then you're ready to roll your own podcast. Most ISPs (Internet service providers) allow you some server space as part of your monthly deal, microphones cost less than a round of drinks, and the necessary software is largely free, so what's stopping you from podcasting?

Defining idea

'Creation comes before distribution – or there will be nothing to distribute.'
AYN RAND, US author

The first step is to write and record your material. Give some thought to your target audience, and remember that even if you only meant it to be heard by the family, once it is on the web it may reach the ears of just about anybody.

Next you need to record to your computer, which means plugging a microphone into the microphone jack and using sound recording software. Audacity (http://audacity.sourceforge.net/) is a popular choice for both PC and Mac but there are dozens of simple sound recording utilities available. The Podcasting News site lists some of the best-known podcasting tools at.

www.podcastingnews.com/topics/Podcasting_Software.html

All podcast audio is in the mp3 format but before you convert to that you should save your precious output at maximum quality so you have a decent original to work from if you want to edit or change it at a later date. Then you can use your sound software to convert (sometimes called 'export as' or 'save as') to mp3 format for broadcasting.

You don't need any programming knowledge to podcast, but in order for people to be able to download your podcast and check for updates you need to create what's called an RSS (for Really Simple Syndication) feed. It sounds complicated, but really it's just a text file that points to your files and describes them. You'll often see an orange button on websites with RSS or XML marked on it – these mean that there is an RSS feed to the content of that site. The easiest way to set up your RSS is to use podcasting or blogging software that will create the file for you (see the excellent range on offer for free at Podcasting News).

Upload the podcast to your website, including the RSS link to it, and don't forget that it's no earthly use unless people know about it so email them or get in touch with one of the podcast portals (www.podcastpickle.com, www.podcastalley.com, etc.) and let them know about it.

Here's an idea for you

When you come to save your broadcast as an mp3 file you are usually offered a number of different 'bit rates' as options. The bit rate means how much information your eventual file will have - the more information the better the quality, but the fatter the file (which makes it clumsy to upload and download). Try to vary your bit rate depending on your needs so that if you are just doing talk radio or readings you can get away with Mono and a rate of 48–56K. Music and talk combined call for 64K Stereo and good-quality listening music should be 128K.

48

Don't take our word for it

Video tutorials on podcasting

As Marshall McLuhan famously said, 'the medium is the message', and it would be a poor advertisement for podcasting if there weren't podcasts that sang their own praises and showed you things to do. Here are some of the best of those podcasts that both talk the talk and walk the walk.

Defining idea

'Today we are beginning to notice that the new media are not just mechanical gimmicks for creating worlds of illusion, but new languages with new and unique powers of expression.'
MARSHALL McLUHAN, media analyst and author.

Four Minutes About Podcasting

Start right here because this cheerful little presentation shows as it tells just why podcasting can be fun, useful and a healthy antidote to mainstream media. Okay, so you may not want to be a 'media hippy', nor might you agree with her definition that podcasting is a space suite for the toxic media environment, but Lisa 'Learning the Lessons of Nixon' Williams does provide a lively intro to why the alternative world of podcasting is good news for all of us. It convinces by virtue of its own fresh enthusiasm and for those looking at enhanced podcasting it also shows how some simple graphics can go a long way if used intelligently. It's a bite-sized bit of video/audio/slideshow too, which makes it suitable for sending on to those as yet unconverted to podcasting.

www.cadence90.com/wp/index.php?p=3548

RocketBoom iTunes walk through

RocketBoom, that most excellent news vlog, also hosts some video walkthroughs of how-to podcasting subjects such as this one, which takes you step by step through using iTunes 4.9 to get podcasts. Because this is shot using screen capture you see in a playback window exactly what you should be doing yourself on screen. Cursor movements and opening menus are all captured making it a lot easier to follow than static step-by-step instructions, including Apple's own introductory tutorials on www.apple.com.

www.rocketboom.com/extra/itunes/

Engadget

Engadget, the online magazine of technology and gadget envy, has illustrated its own how-to articles with a podcast tutorial both on getting podcasts and on making your own. It's quite endearing because the folks at Engadget made their tutorial as their own first podcast and so are picking it up as they go, just like the rest of us.

www.engadget.com/entry/5843952395227141/

Here's an idea for you

Podcast About The Podcast may sound like a dog chasing its tail but this is from Michael Geoghegan, the man behind the highly successful Reel Reviews movie site. Taking a break from his normal roundup of the great and the good on the big screen, Michael instead turns his attention to the medium itself and talks about how he goes about putting together the podcast that his listeners subscribe to – a relaxed and informative little 'making of' podcast. It would be nice to hear a few more from other established podcasters.

http://homepage.mac.com/mgeoghegan/PODCASTS/Reel-
About_The_Podcast.mp3

49

Podcast pro

Tips for taking a step up the slick scale

As with so many things, getting started in podcasting is a piece of pod but getting good at it means investing time, thought and money. Here are some places to start.

Defining idea

'A professional writer is an amateur who didn't quit.'
RICHARD BACH, author of *Jonathan Livingstone Seagull*

The studio

A full-on professional recording studio is beyond the reach of most of us but there's a lot you can do to improve the environment where you record your podcast. Think carefully about where to work: a huge hall will result in tomb-like acoustics while a tiled bathroom will bounce sound back at you and can be off-putting. If you're really serious about this you could always put up acoustic damping in the den, but one shortcut to improved sound is simply to hang up duvets and sheets around your recording space.

The microphone

You pay peanuts, you get podcasts fit for apes. The first thing to splash the cash on is your microphone because it has the most direct effect on your sound quality. Mikes can cost as little as a bacon roll, or as much as a Rolls Royce but if there's one thing you're going to smash the piggy bank for then this is it. Try a look at the range on display at any one time at the Podcasting News microphone guide:

http://www.podcastingnews.com/category/Large_Stand-Mount_Condenser_Microphones.htm

The mixer

If you thought a good mixer was a ginger ale, a party goer or a party goer with a lot of drinks inside them then it's time to do some homework. The role of the mixer is to allow you to adjust the different levels of the elements of sound, and to balance them out to your satisfaction. Mixers now often come with digital effects like reverb (careful not to overdo the common ones) and different numbers of separate sound channels available, but as even twelve-channel mixers are now relatively cheap you are unlikely to demand more than your mixer can deliver.

The audio interface

This is the bit that takes your beautifully mixed mike input and feeds it into a computer. It can be as simple as a cable with a plug at each end, or it can be a separate box that handles high-quality digitisation (converting your audio sound to computer signals).

The computer

Ah yes, you start to use better quality raw material, add transition effects, background sound, jingles, and reverb and before you know it your trusty old workhorse machine will slow to a halt. More memory, more hard drive space, and top whack processors are required – and that's before you move on from your old copy of Audacity and start to yearn dreamily for top-end audio software.

Here's an idea for you

Since you've gone beyond the spoken voice, you'll now need music to provide entertainment, transitions, backgrounds and 'stings' for your show. This risks falling foul of copyright rules so it's time to get familiar with 'podsafe' music. Try Magnatune, Creative Commons, the Association of Music Podcasting or Podsafe Audio for music you can use without fearing the copyright police's knock on the door.

http:/magnatune.com/
http:/creativecommons.org/
http:/musicpodcasting.org/
http:/podsafeaudio.com/

50

Podcasting for fun and profit

Getting sponsorship and/or advertising

As podcasting has gone from amateur audio blogging to the playground of companies like Disney and Bravo, the question of advertising and revenue was never far away. How to make a buck with podcasting isn't clear cut, but already there are those looking for ways to make it work.

Defining idea

'Advertising is the greatest art form of the twentieth century.'
MARSHALL McLUHAN, media analyst and author.

Most podcasts were put together without a thought for earning money and they revelled in their amateur approach. However, now that podcasting has picked up momentum and become recognised as a medium to be reckoned with, there are inevitable experiments into how exactly to make it pay. In many ways it reflects the early days of the Internet itself and just as some websites tried (usually unsuccessfully) to sell their content so there are certain podcasters

(Rush Limbaugh stands out) charging for subscriptions to their shows. For most, however, that doesn't seem like the way forward and as the number of people tuning in to podcasts increases (with help from the launch of the pod-friendly iTunes 4.9) so does interest in traffic, click rates, and getting brands in front of consumer 'eyeballs'.

Sponsorship deals are already being done but one of the problems faced by the media moguls is that once a podcast is downloaded it's hard to know how many times it is then played. Something downloaded once and played once will obviously have less appeal compared with something people listen to over and over. Currently, sponsorships usually involve short embedded audio ads and buttons or banner adverts on the site, such as Lexus and its sponsorship of KCRW (a Californian radio station) podcasts. Marketeers will increasingly turn to corporate podcasts as branding excercises – Purina pet food has already got its own podcast on pet care and condom maker Durex is reportedly keen to place itself in podcasts too.

The big hurdle, then, as it was in standard web advertising, is likely to be accurate measurement of the exposure the advertiser/sponsor gets among customers. Because of that, anyone looking to make money from their own podcasts would be wise to start by turning to one of the service companies that provide reliable monitoring (such as Feedburner – *www.feedburner.com*).

Here's an idea for you

It'll be one podcaster in a thousand that turns a profit from their pod but for those who feel that they have compelling enough content to attract advertisers then you can get an idea of just how it would work by looking at one of the dedicated podcast advertising engines springing up. CastFire, for example, automatically combines intros, outros, and interstitial (in between) adverts for podcasts, based on keywords that tie that podcast to likely consumer interest. It hosts the media, analyses the traffic, and pays you for every download that includes advertising. Take a peek at the shape of things to come at:

www.castfire.com

51

Good morning campers!

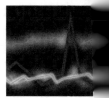

Putting your hospital/community radio onto podcast

We've already seen that putting together podcast radio is cheap and simple, but how do you go about taking an existing hospital or community station and bringing it to the pod party?

Defining idea

'It is not so much our friends' help that helps us as the confident knowledge that they will help us.'
EPICURUS

Podcasting is episodic whereas radio tends to be always on and so the transition from local radio to podcasting is more about selecting the right content than it is about managing the technology. From the creative point of view, you need digital audio, which means digitising your own content either through a mixer (see IDEA 49, *Podcast Pro*) or, at the very least, recording it to a computer via a microphone. You may also want to consider encouraging your listeners to send in their digital input (many phones and computers can now record voice straight to mp3 files) to do vox pop pieces without the hassle of a phone switchboard. From there you'll need to use an editor to splice up all your fabulous content into programme-sized pieces.

The next step, that of hosting the content, writing and validating the XML that will make it possible for others to subscribe, is usually the one that new podcasters baulk at. I'm guessing that you're coming at this from a radio background, not a computer one, and so while recording and editing are second (okay, maybe third) nature, setting up an RSS feed sounds like rocket science. Don't panic – get help. If you want to do it yourself, then go to TypePad (www.typepad.com) or Blogger (www.blogger.com), which have the tools to turn your mp3 into a podcast. If you're still unsure, there's a step-by-step guide to creating a podcast from Blogger at:

www.forret.com/blog/2004/10/how-to-podcast-with-blogger-and.html

If you're thinking of going even bigger than that and maybe one day trying to encourage advertising or sponsors then you'll need more complex tools, including detailed analysis of the popularity of your podcast. For that kind of service you need a podcast service company such as FeedBurner (www.feedburner.com) which will manage the RSS for you and help you publicise your show and analyse the uptake. Many of the services are free; others are on a sliding scale so you only pay as you start to need more sophisticated tools.

Here's an idea for you

Happy to create your mp3 files but uncomfortable about setting up the XML needed to have others subscribe and automatically download? Then you could try a professional podcasting service that will link to your webcasts, advertise your podcast to the podcast portals and handle the server traffic as punters beat a path to your digital door. At the moment, one such service, Prestopod, is trying out a beta form of just that, with the agreeable twist that while they are themselves in a trial period, you don't have to pay anything for the service. Take a look and find out what a podcasting service could do for your fledgling radio station at:

www.prestopod.com

52

Let's be careful out there, people

A legal guide to putting out your podcast

While podcasting still doesn't quite rank up there with bank robbing, white slave trading, or serving short measures in pubs, it can still lead decent law-abiding people (such as yourself) down the slippery slope to illegality.

Defining idea

'I fought the law, and the law won.'
JOE STRUMMER esq. (and the Clash).

The most obvious area of risk is copyright infringement. Appropriate as it might be to have the 'Chariots of Fire' as background music to your school sports day podcast, that remains unlicensed usage as far as the artist and record company are concerned. Even if they don't actually track you down and kick your door in (not as unlikely as you might think these days) you will probably have broken the terms of your contract with your web host by using their server to distribute unauthorised music mp3s. At the very least they may decide to suspend your service to protect themselves and that's the end of your podcast fame. The best answer is to make sure that you're decent, legal, and sweet smelling. So bear in mind that there are only three ways of having legal music in your podcast:

- Buy a licence (no, really);
- Use royalty free music – most classical music falls into this category, for example, but check for yourself to make sure;
- Make your own music – you write it, you hum it; however bad it may be, it's yours and you won't have to hide under the table waiting for the knock on the door.

Aside from the copyright issue it's important to respect the lines between what you want to broadcast as an individual, and what your employers or local law agency may deem acceptable. It often seems that anything goes online, but as Mum always told you, 'It's only funny until someone gets hurt.' In the US, podcasters have already been fired from their jobs because their podcasts were deemed dodgy. If you are identified as the mastermind behind the Lesbian Lavatory Lust podcast and yet your day job is as the editor of the parish newsletter you may find your employers think you are bringing them into disrepute by association. A bit of common sense comes in handy too – a surprising number of podcasters have ended up being sued because they chose to mouth off about their jobs, giving out confidential information in the process. Podcasting may seem like a harmless hobby but legally it is publishing and that means that the laws of slander and professional confidence apply.

Here's an idea for you

Podcasting is basically blogging (writing online diaries) with added music, talk and funny noises. So go take a peek at the *Legal Guide for Bloggers* from the Electronic Frontiers Foundation. The *Guide* is intended as 'a basic roadmap to the legal issues you may confront as a blogger, to let you know you have rights, and to encourage you to blog freely with the knowledge that your legitimate speech is protected.' It's not that hard and fast on law outside the US, but it is very useful as a reminder of some of the dos and don'ts you might otherwise overlook.

EFF: **Legal Guide for Bloggers** – *www.eff.org/bloggers/lg/*

If you enjoyed this book, you may also like...

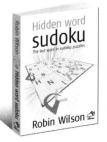

Hidden word sudoku
The last word in sudoku puzzles
by Robin Wilson

Rudoku
The rudest sudoku word puzzles ever*
by Hugh Janus

See the next four pages for special offers on these and other select titles in the **52 Brilliant Ideas** series.

* No. We really mean it. They're pretty rude so buyers beware.

CALL US A BUNCH OF PUBLISHING PUSHOVERS BUT...

Get 25%** off on these select titles direct from Infinite Ideas.

	Qty	Title	RRP
Inspired fun		Hidden word sudoku	£4.99
		Rudoku	£4.99
		Getting away with it	£6.99
52 Brilliant Ideas		Win at the gym	£12.99
		Websites that work	£12.99
		Detox your finances	£12.99
		Secrets of wine	£12.99
		Inspired creative writing	£12.99
		Sub-total	
		LESS PUSHOVER DISCOUNT OF 25%	
		P&P £0.50 per book	
		Grand total	

For full details of these books and others in the **52 Brilliant Ideas** series please visit www.52brilliantideas.com.

See over for details on how to place your order.

**Offer is good until you decide to use this book as a door stop.

Ref: PODAD06

How to place your order

Name: ....

Delivery address: ....

....

....

....

E-mail: ....

Telephone: ....

(We never give details to 3rd parties nor will we bombard you with lots of junk mail!)

By post

Fill in all the relevant details, cut this page out and send along with a cheque made payable to Infinite Ideas.

Send to: Infinite Ideas, 36 St Giles, Oxford OX1 3LD, UK

Credit card orders over the telephone

Call +44 (0) 1865 514 888. Please quote reference PODAD 06.

Any questions please call +44 (0) 1865 514 888 or e-mail info@infideas.com.

www.52brilliantideas.com

Getting away with it

Shortcuts to the things you don't really deserve

Edited by Steve Shipside

Win at the gym

Secrets of fitness and health success

By Steve Shipside

Web sites that work

Secrets from winning web sites

By Jon Smith

Start-up CD

This mini-CD contains a selection of a few of the best podcatchers for you so you don't even have to download them. You will also find useful links to some of the best podcast sites out there. The CD is compatible with Windows 2000 and XP and Mac-OSX.

Insert the mini CD into the central recess of any tray-loading CD-Rom drive. The CD will launch automatically in Windows. To access the software from a Mac select the disk on your desktop and then double click the 'PP' icon. We apologise but this disk will not work in slot-loading drives.

If the CD is missing from this book please contact Infinite Ideas by emailing info@infideas.com or calling +44 1865 514888.